Fortnite

by Bill Loguidice

for
dummies®
A Wiley Brand

Fortnite® For Dummies®

Published by: **John Wiley & Sons, Inc.**, 111 River Street, Hoboken, NJ 07030-5774, www.wiley.com

Copyright © 2019 by John Wiley & Sons, Inc., Hoboken, New Jersey

Published simultaneously in Canada

For general information on our other products and services, please contact our Customer Care Department within the U.S. at 877-762-2974, outside the U.S. at 317-572-3993, or fax 317-572-4002. For technical support, please visit https://hub.wiley.com/community/support/dummies.

Wiley publishes in a variety of print and electronic formats and by print-on-demand. Some material included with standard print versions of this book may not be included in e-books or in print-on-demand. If this book refers to media such as a CD or DVD that is not included in the version you purchased, you may download this material at http://booksupport.wiley.com. For more information about Wiley products, visit www.wiley.com.

Library of Congress Control Number: 2019942817

ISBN 978-1-119-60610-9 (pbk); ISBN 978-1-119-60608-6 (ebk); ISBN 978-1-119-60612-3 (ebk)

Manufactured in the United States of America

V10011722_062819

Contents at a Glance

Table of Contents

Introduction

I f you like fast-paced, competitive online action games with ever-evolving variety and creativity to spare, Fortnite, from Epic Games, is for you. It's one of the most popular free games of all-time, with hundreds of millions of registered players world-wide across a variety of platforms. You'll never be lacking in new friends to play with or against!

There are three main Fortnite modes. The first mode is Save the World, which was the original version of the game and focuses on surviving against the elements and enemies in various missions that make up a campaign. The second is Battle Royale, where groups of up to 100 players compete to be the last team or person standing and is the mode that made Fortnite what it is today. The third and final is Creative, a sandbox game mode where players are free to create anything they want on their own island, including battle arenas, race courses, labyrinths, and more, and where the best creations can go on to be featured in the Hub.

Although there's a lot to the Fortnite experience, as long as you keep in mind that it's always a game with clear objectives that encourages creativity in reaching them, you'll have fun playing. While reading or referencing *Fortnite For Dummies*, you can apply every bit of game and gameplay information you need to start getting the most out of this cultural phenomenon.

About This Book

This book assumes no knowledge of Fortnite, and it can guide you from registering a free account to competing in your first match to building your best defensive structures, and so much more.

Although Fortnite has a massive community of players, including high-profile celebrities and regular professional gaming tournaments, as well as a huge pop culture impact with everything from dances to apparel, *Fortnite For Dummies* focuses primarily on the game itself, and the Battle Royale mode in particular. The information you learn will help you enjoy and succeed in all modes, however, and is a great way to get a leg up on exploring the greater Fortnite universe outside of the game.

Fortnite For Dummies is a helpful resource for new Fortnite players to gain a foothold and then momentum in the game, as well as recall information they may have otherwise forgotten. Though this book goes only so far in giving strategic guidance, leaving what is at its heart a game of discovery to be revealed through play, you can find quite a bit of information in this book on many of Fortnite's more complex and interesting systems and components.

Because Fortnite is constantly evolving and works around the concept of seasons, this book is accurate to Season 8. Because later updates and seasons are unlikely to change the core game mechanics, this book encompasses most of Fortnite's main features.

Foolish Assumptions

Rather than try to consider every single type of reader who might pick up this book, I've made certain assumptions about you, the reader:

>> You have a computer, console, or mobile device and know the basics of using it.

>> Your computer, console, or mobile device is connected to the Internet.

>> Your Internet connection is stable and fast enough to play competitive online games.

>> Your computer, console, or mobile device has enough storage space available to download, run, and keep Fortnite up-to-date.

Icons Used in This Book

I've placed various icons in the margins of this book to point out specific information you may find useful:

TIP

This icon calls attention to any tip or trick that you can use to enhance gameplay.

This icon emphasizes points that you should attempt to retain in your memory. If you can remember these points, you'll be a more successful player.

REMEMBER

If you see this icon, pay attention! Warnings can prevent you from making a mistake that can be detrimental to your Fortnite experience.

WARNING

You can safely skip this overly nerdy or technical information. However, because it deserved a place in this book, you may be interested in reading it.

TECHNICAL STUFF

Beyond the Book

In addition to the material in the print or ebook you're reading right now, this product also comes with some access-anywhere goodies on the web. No matter how well you understand Fortnite concepts, you'll likely come across a few questions where you don't have a clue. To get this material, simply go to www.dummies.com and search for "*Fortnite For Dummies* Cheat Sheet" in the Search box.

Where to Go from Here

Reading *Fortnite For Dummies* from cover-to-cover provides a lot of useful information, but you can just as easily skip around to find specific topics of interest. If you're new to Fortnite and you want to know what the game is all about, read Chapters 1 through 3 and skim most of the other ones. They delve into more detail than is necessary for a first-time player. You can always visit those chapters later.

If you're a little more experienced in Fortnite and want to deepen your understanding, you can skim the first three chapters and then find some more interesting topics later in the book. Also be sure to check out Chapters 9 and 10, which provide tips for getting even more out of your Fortnite experience.

Occasionally, Wiley's technology books are updated. If this book has technical updates, they'll be posted at

https://www.dummies.com/go/fortnitefdupdates

Chapter **1**

Entering the Fortnite Universe

ven though it's one of countless online shooting and survival games, Fortnite still manages to distinguish itself with its unique mix of variety and fun. No two matches are ever the same, and it seems like there's always something new to discover. The fact that you can customize your in-game avatar's appearance, weapons, and, yes, dance moves in all kinds of wacky ways explains at least part of the game's charm and why it has such broad appeal. It's no wonder that it's consistently the most watched game, often by a gap of hundreds of thousands of viewers, on live streaming video website, Twitch.tv!

In *Save the World* mode, you and three other players, either humans or computer-generated teammates, work towards a common goal on various missions in a storm-ravaged Earth where 98 percent of the population has vanished. In this mode, you're attacked by a variety of zombie-like monsters referred to as husks, which seem to explain where all those missing humans have gone. Of course, you'll encounter plenty of other monsters along the way, so you'll need to build structures, set traps, and gather loot to help your cause.

Battle Royale is the most popular game mode and the one Fortnite is most closely associated with. You play alone or in groups to compete in 100 player battles to be the last person or team standing. Most of what you need to succeed in Battle Royale can be applied to the two other major game modes and vice-versa.

In *Creative* mode, you have access to a private island where you can assemble and upgrade structures and manipulate objects as you see fit. You can invite friends to your island and try different game types, including racing and obstacle courses. Epic Games chooses the best creations to be featured in the Creative mode's Hub, but you can also enter your own codes to check out the creations of your choice!

This chapter explains how to get started in Fortnite, how to choose your platform, the basics of the virtual currency known as V-Bucks, what Seasons mean, and how cross-platform play works.

Choosing PC/Mac, Console, or Mobile

Although Fortnite originally started out as a PC exclusive, the game's framework was designed in such a way that it made ports to other platforms practical. These other platforms include Apple Mac computers, iOS and Android mobile devices, and the Sony PlayStation 4, Microsoft Xbox One, and Nintendo Switch consoles.

As of this writing, the PC, Mac, PlayStation 4, and Xbox One platforms support every available game mode. Players on iOS, Android, and Nintendo Switch systems, on the other hand, do not have access to the player-versus-environment game mode, Save the World.

There are other differences between the various platforms, as explained in the following subsections.

Considering PC/Mac

A PC or Mac computer is an ideal Fortnite platform. It has every game mode, as shown in Figure 1-1, and you can choose to play either with a traditional keyboard/mouse combination or with a game controller.

FIGURE 1-1: Game mode options on the PC version of Fortnite.

Refer to Table 1-1 for minimum and recommended system requirements. If your computer is closer to the minimum than recommended requirements, check out Chapter 2 for settings you can adjust to tweak performance.

TABLE 1-1 **PC and Mac Minimum and Recommended System Requirements**

System Component	Minimum	Recommended
Operating System	Windows 7/8/10 64-bit or Mac OSX Sierra	Same
CPU	Processor Core i3 2.4 Ghz	Processor Core i5 2.8 Ghz
Memory	4 GB RAM	8 GB RAM
Video Card	Intel HD 4000	Nvidia GTX 660 or AMD Radeon HD 7870 equivalent DX11 GPU
Video Memory	Shared	2 GB VRAM

Considering iOS/Android

On a mobile device, Fortnite can be a bit more challenging to play than it is on some of the other platforms, but it's still a great way to game on-the-go or when your computer or console is otherwise tied up. Although there's limited support for game controllers, Fortnite on iOS and Android is designed around the touchscreen experience, so you don't need anything other than the smartphone or tablet you already have to enjoy the experience.

For Apple iOS devices, you'll need iOS11 or greater. If you want to play on an iPhone, you'll need an iPhone SE, 6S, 7, 8, or X series device or later. If you want to play on an iPad, you'll need an iPad Mini 4, iPad Air 2, 2017, Pro or later. Naturally, the larger the screen, the better the experience.

As of this writing, Fortnite support on Android devices is still limited. In fact, Epic Games has chosen to avoid distributing the game through the Google Play Store, instead making it available only on its own website through a Fortnite Installer program, as well as on Samsung's app store and Game Launcher for owners of Samsung devices.

WARNING

For safety reasons, only download the Android version of the game from the Epic Games website or Samsung's app store. Any other source that claims to have the game is likely to try to install an unrelated program that might compromise the security of your smartphone or tablet.

You will need to request the installer from the Epic Games website, or, if you have a Samsung device, from Samsung's app store, to determine whether your device is compatible. Generally speaking, newer, name brand devices that feature at least 64-bit Android 8.0, 3GB of RAM, and a GPU with Adreno 530, Mali-H71 MP20, or Mali-G72 MP12 have a good chance of being compatible.

Considering PlayStation 4/Xbox One

The only other way to get the full Fortnite experience outside of a PC is on either PlayStation 4 or Xbox One. Fortnite is compatible with all PlayStation 4 and Xbox One consoles, but, as with many games, visual and other performance improvements may exist when played on the PlayStation 4 Pro or Xbox One X. Regardless of the version of console you play it on, all Fortnite features are available and accessible from the standard gamepad. If you want a more PC-like experience, keyboard and mouse support is also available for both consoles.

For Xbox One owners, you will need to have an Xbox Live account and an active Xbox Live Gold membership to participate in the game. For PlayStation 4 owners, you do not need a PlayStation Plus membership to play the game.

Considering Nintendo Switch

The Nintendo Switch is one of the most popular Fortnite platforms. Thanks to the Switch's unique ability to play on the go as well on a TV, it combines some of the best features of the more advanced console and portable mobile experiences. The Switch's standard control configuration for its Joy-Cons is available, but you can also use the Pro Controller or Motion Controls should those suit your needs better.

For Nintendo Switch owners, you do not need Nintendo Switch Online to play the game.

Registering a Fortnite Account

Before you can enjoy Fornite, you should register an Epic Games account. Although you can go straight to downloading the game on your platform of choice and registering an account from there, going through the Epic Games website from a computer's web browser gives you the most options, including the ability to more easily associate additional accounts.

TIP

Epic Games is opening its cross-platform game services that power Fortnite to other developers, so it's likely that your Epic Games account will become even more useful in the future.

Follow these steps to register an account on your computer:

1. Go to https://www.epicgames.com/fortnite/.

The Epic Games Fortnite home page opens.

2. Click the Get Fortnite button or menu option.

The How Would You Like to Play? screen appears.

3. **Click PC/Mac.**

The Create Account page appears.

Clicking PlayStation, Xbox, or Switch takes you to the Fortnite information and download page on the respective platform's digital store. Clicking Mobile takes you to Step 4.

4. **Fill out all the information requested in the text boxes. If you have their respective login info handy, you can also save some time by using your PlayStation, Xbox, Switch, Facebook, or Google accounts as your sign-in by clicking on their respective icons above the text boxes.**

Although checking off "I would like to receive latest news and information on this product." is optional, it's recommended you do so. The frequency of emails is relatively low, and it's an easy way to stay up-to-date on some of the latest Fornite-related news.

5. **Click Create Account.**

The download now begins. If you do not wish to install the PC/Mac version of Fortnite at this time, cancel the download.

With your Epic Games account created, you are now ready to download and install the game on your platform of choice. Check out the subsection that follows to find out how to associate additional accounts with your Epic Games account, or the next section for information on installing Fortnite.

Associating Additional Accounts

You can link your Github, Twitch, Xbox, PlayStation Network, and Nintendo Switch accounts to your Epic Games account. This can make using those other services and platforms with Fortnite easier since they will already be associated with your Epic Games account. To link additional accounts, do the following:

1. **Use your web browser to go to** https://fortnite.com.

The Fortnite home page opens.

2. **Click Sign In on the upper right of the page.**

The Do You Already Play Fortnite? prompt appears.

3. **Click Yes.**

The What Do You Play Fortnite On? page appears.

4. **Click PC/Mac.**

5. **Enter the email address and password associated with your Epic Games account.**

6. **Click Sign In.**

   You are now signed in.

7. **Click your login name in the upper right of the screen and select Account, as shown in Figure 1-2.**

   The Personal Info screen appears.

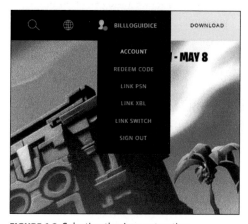

FIGURE 1-2: Selecting the Account option.

8. **Click Connected Accounts on the left-hand side of the screen.**

9. **Click Connect under any or all of the relevant listed accounts to associate those logins with your Epic Games account.**

Installing Fortnite

After you have a registered Epic Games account, you can install Fortnite on the platform of your choice.

Installing on PC/Mac

The process for installing on PC or Mac computers is similar. Follow these steps:

1. **Use your web browser to go to** https://fortnite.com.

The Fortnite home page opens.

2. **Click the Download button on the upper right of the page, as shown in Figure 1-3.**

The How Would You Like to Play? Screen appears.

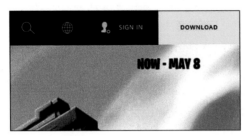

FIGURE 1-3: The Download button on the Fortnite home page.

3. **Click PC/Mac.**

The Create Account page appears.

4. **Click Sign In.**

5. **Enter the email address and password associated with your Epic Games account.**

6. **Click Sign In.**

The Thank You for Downloading screen appears and your download begins.

7. **Save the Epic Games Installer to the location of your choice.**

8. **Go to the Epic Game Installer's save location and run the program.**

Follow the remaining instructions to install the Epic Games Launcher and Fortnite.

Installing on iOS/Android

On your iOS device, visit the App Store and search for Fortnite. Tap on Get to begin the installation process.

As of this writing, Fortnite for Android is still in the invitation-only process. To install this version of the game, go to https://fortnite.com/android either on a computer or your Android device and follow the instructions.

Installing on console

PlayStation 4, Xbox One, and Nintendo Switch owners can install Fortnite from the respective online stores directly from those consoles. If you own PlayStation 4, visit the PlayStation Store. If you own Xbox One, visit the Xbox Marketplace. If you own Nintendo Switch, visit the Nintendo eShop.

Regardless of console, Fortnite is only available as a digital download and not as a retail game on disc or cartridge. If you do see a retail version of Fortnite, it will only contain a redemption code for the digital version of the game, as well as any other bonuses, like V-Bucks.

Getting to Know the Game Options and Modes

Save the World, Battle Royale, and Creative are the three main game options. The most popular game option, Battle Royale, has a selection of regular game modes, as well as a selection of limited time modes, or LTMs, which, as the name suggests, appear as an option only for a set period of time before they are replaced by something else.

Regular game modes form the core Battle Royale play experience and feature Solo, Duos, and Squads. LTMs feature different weapons, win conditions, and more, but they are usually a Solo, Duos, or Squads game type. There's also Playground mode under Battle Royale, which is a more limited and restricted form of Creative.

Understanding Save the World

Save the World, which is available to PC/Mac, PlayStation 4, and Xbox One players, is what is known as a Player versus Environment, or PvE, game. Unlike its more popular offshoot, Battle Royale, which is a Player versus Player, or PvP, game, Save the World is a cooperative, mission-based game of survival in a destructible world. You play with up to three other people on a randomly generated map to fight against a storm, rescue survivors, build structures, craft weapons, find loot, and upgrade and expand a shield device to protect your base of operations.

WARNING

As of this writing, Save the World is still in early access and requires a payment of $39.99 for the Standard Edition of the game mode, and $59.99 for the Deluxe Edition. Epic Games has stated that they intend to make this mode free to play some time in 2019.

The skills you learn from playing Save the World can be applied to the rest of the Fortnite experience and vice-versa. For instance, in all game modes you use a pickaxe to knock down existing structures and collect resources like wood or metal. Similarly, you use those harvested materials in all game modes to build and repair structures like walls, floors, and stairs, although only in Save the World can you upgrade structures.

As of this writing, Save the World costs money to play, but, like Battle Royale and Creative, is expected to go free some time in 2019 once Epic Games feels the game mode is more developed.

Understanding Battle Royale

Battle Royale is the Player versus Player, or PvP, game mode that put Fortnite on the map. You and 99 other players start off in a flying battle bus, find a landing spot, then race to collect materials, weapons, and other loot to defeat the other players.

For the Solo game modes, it's you against 99 other players. (See Figure 1-4.) For Duos, you can team up with a friend (or friendly stranger) against 49 other teams of two. In Duos, your partner can revive you if you're wounded. For Squads, you join a team of three other players and try and be the last of 25 four-player teams standing. Squads is usually Fortnite's most popular mode.

FIGURE 1-4: The beginning of a Solo game on Nintendo Switch, shortly after landing.

Playground, which was formerly an LTE, or Limited Time Event, but is now a permanent addition, lets you play solo or with up to three other players for a more restriction-free play experience. You get a much longer time limit than with other modes, allowing you to more freely explore the map, harvest materials, build things, search for chests, and more. You can still fight, but only against your other three friends.

With Duos, Squads, and Playground, you need to decide between Fill or Don't Fill. With Fill, if you have less than the number of players needed to form the required team size in a particular mode, the game will automatically match you up with other players. If you choose Don't Fill and don't have a full team, you will be going up against other, properly sized groups, at a disadvantage. Don't Fill is an unusual option to say the least, but it is an excellent example of how incredibly customizable the Fortnite experience really is.

Understanding Creative

In Creative mode, you gain access to your own private island, where you can pretty much design or do whatever you want, including inviting your friends over for some playtesting. You'll have all kinds of materials at your disposal, so you can do more than just build structures. In fact, this mode is designed around the concept of creating new game types with the Fortnite engine, including deathmatches, races, soccer matches, skate parks, arenas, and more, as in the example in Figure 1-5.

FIGURE 1-5: The beginning of Creative mode on PlayStation 4.

You can save and load your creations, so you're free to be as creative, or destructive, as you like. You can even enter special codes to load the amazing creations of others, which range from elaborately designed adventure mazes to playable mini golf courses and everything in-between. The possibilities really are staggering with the versatile Fortnite game engine.

Understanding V-Bucks

Although Fortnite is free to play, it's more accurately described as *freemium*, a portmanteau of "free" and "premium." What this means is that the base product is provided free of charge, but money, in the form of in-game currency known as V-Bucks, is charged for additional features.

Fortunately, in Fortnite's case, most of what costs V-Bucks are cosmetic items like character skins, pickaxes, gliders, emotes (gestures or dance moves), contrails (skydiving trails), emoticons (in-game emojis), backpacks, and sprays.

TIP

Cosmetics offer no in-game advantages, but they're still a big part of Fortnite. The more cosmetics you have available, the more personalized you can make your character and overall in-game experience. It's all part of the fun and a great way to support continued development of the game.

Although you can unlock V-Bucks and quite a few cosmetics free-of-charge through dedicated play, you'll likely still need to make a direct V-Bucks purchase on occasion to acquire some of the more interesting items, or to acquire a popular season-specific rewards bundle known as a *Battle Pass*.

Purchasing V-Bucks

All V-Bucks purchases take place through the in-game Store tab, as shown in the example in Figure 1-6, or the respective Play-Station 4 or Xbox One digital marketplaces. As of this writing, a minimum 1,000 V-Bucks purchase costs $9.99. You can also buy larger bundles of V-Bucks, which come with bonus V-Bucks. For instance, 2,500 V-Bucks plus a 300 V-Buck bonus for $24.99 or 10,000 V-Bucks plus a 3,500 V-Buck bonus for $99.99.

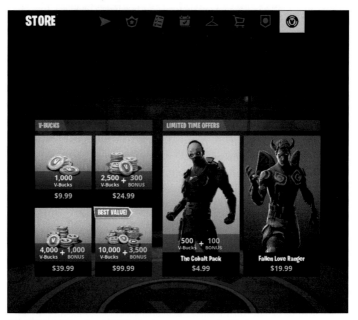

FIGURE 1-6: V-Bucks options in-game on an Apple iPad.

WARNING

If you see offers online for free V-Bucks, it's probably a scam. Visiting websites or clicking links that claim to offer free V-Bucks or V-Buck generating tools is unsafe. It's best to purchase V-Bucks directly from the in-game store, or, if you're playing on a PlayStation 4 or an Xbox One, their official digital stores.

It's important to keep in mind that V-Bucks purchased on one platform may not be redeemable on other platforms. Purchase V-Bucks on the platform you plan to spend it on. Fortunately, after spending your V-Bucks on that specific platform for cosmetics or a Battle Pass, those items will then be available to you on any other platform you play Fortnite on as long as use the same login.

Spending V-Bucks

V-Bucks can be spent in Save the World, Battle Royale, or Creative. Keep in mind, however, that items bought in Save the World don't transfer to Battle Royale/Creative, and vice-versa.

In Save the World, you can purchase Llama Pinata card packs that contain weapon and trap schematics, as well as new Heroes and more. In Battle Royale and Creative you can purchase new customization items for your Hero, glider, or pickaxe.

Fortnite works on the concept of themed seasons, like Season 8's pirate-related theme. Buying a Battle Pass for the current season, which costs 950 V-Bucks as of this writing, allows you to unlock season-specific rewards the more you play. You can also level up faster with a Battle Pass by completing Weekly Challenges to unlock additional rewards like outfits, wraps, emotes, pets, and other exclusive cosmetics.

If you're in a particular rush to get an initial set of season-specific cosmetics, you can purchase what is called a Battle Bundle, which costs 2,800 V-Bucks as of this writing, and includes the Battle Pass and an instant unlock for the next 25 tiers of experience points, cosmetics, and V-Bucks. You can also buy up to 100 tiers, each for 150 V-Bucks. Otherwise, to unlock over 100 rewards worth over 25,000 V-Bucks, you'll need to play a particular season for at least 75 to 150 total hours.

Getting to Know Seasons

Seasons are Fortnite's way of introducing new features and cosmetics, the latter of which is typically tied to a larger theme, on a regular schedule. Because each season lasts only around 10 weeks, it's a great way to keep the game fresh and encourage its players to play as much as possible to unlock all the cosmetics they can before they're no longer available.

Fortnite's Battle Royale reward system, the Battle Pass, is closely associated with its seasons. However, the Battle Pass itself wasn't even introduced until Season 2, based as it was on the progression system introduced in Season 1. And although the Battle Pass costs V-Bucks, you can still unlock a subset of items for no cost with the Free Pass. Nevertheless, many players and references often conflate both the Battle Pass and Free Pass under "Battle Pass."

TIP

Seasons can sometimes bring big changes to the map. Keep an eye out for unusual happenings in a particular season. For instance, in Season 3, a mysterious meteor appeared in the sky. This meteor destroyed the map area known as Dusty Depot, turning it into Dusty Divot for Season 4, as well as creating smaller craters throughout other areas.

Although it's not necessarily critical to know when past seasons ran, what their themes were, or what they introduced, it's still interesting to see how the game has progressed, giving some sense of where future seasons may be headed. Check out Table 1-2 for the highlights of Seasons 1–8.

TABLE 1-2 **Highlights for Seasons 1–8**

Season	Schedule	Theme	Key Additions
1	October 25, 2017–December 13, 2017	None	Leaderboard, toggle targeting
2	December 14, 2017–February 21, 2018	Medieval	The Battle Pass, Map additions, emotes, emoticons
3	February 22, 2018–April 30, 2018	Outer Space	Loading screens, weekly challenges, contrails
4	May 1, 2018–July 12, 2018	Urban Super Heroes	Jet packs, hop rocks, shopping carts, sprays, weekly loading screens, progressive outfits
5	July 12, 2018–September 27, 2018	Worlds Collide	Toys, desert biome, rifts for teleportation
6	September 27, 2018–December 6, 2018	Darkness Rises	Pets, music
7	December 6, 2018–February 28, 2019	Winter Wonderland	Creative mode, wraps, animated loading screens, X-4 Stormwing plane
8	February 28, 2019–May 8, 2019	Pirates	Jungle biome, volcano, lava, pirate cannons, pirate campsites, buried treasure

Understanding Cross-Platform Play

A typical problem with online videogames is the issue of bridging platforms. Your friends or family members may own the same game as you, but if they own a different system, you're unlikely to be able to play with or against each other. Fortnite is the very first game that solves this problem by allowing cross-platform between today's computers, consoles, and mobile devices, with the last holdout, Sony, finally getting with the program and allowing an exception for Fortnite on PlayStation 4.

Regardless of the platform you're playing on, as mentioned earlier in this chapter, you need an Epic Games account for cross-platform play, as well as to synchronize your progress between systems. If you or your friends and family are signed up only on a specific platform's account, then that account will need to be linked to an Epic Games account to join in on the cross-platform fun. All but Solo mode games, which, by definition, exclude teams, are available for cross-platform play.

IN THIS CHAPTER

» **Selecting a game mode**

» **Getting to know the lobby**

» **Adjusting settings**

» **Getting to know the controls**

» **Buying accessories**

Chapter **2**

Customizing Settings, Gameplay, and Controls

N ow that you have a better idea of all that Fortnite involves, it's time to get to know the game's finer details. As with most of its other features, Fortnite's in-game settings and control options have an amazing variety of configurability . All of these in-game settings and control options are available from the lobby, which appears after selecting a game mode and reviewing the News screen.

Selecting a Game Mode

When you first start Fortnite on a PC, Mac, PlayStation 4, or Xbox One, you're presented with three main options: Save the World, Battle Royale, and Creative. This screen is shown in Figure 2-1.

Selecting Save the World takes you straight to that play mode, which is separate from Battle Royale and Creative. Selecting Battle Royale or Creative takes you to the pre-lobby screen, referred to as the News screen, shown in Figure 2-2. This is also the first options screen that appears for iOS, Android, and Nintendo Switch players.

FIGURE 2-1: Game mode selection on Xbox One.

FIGURE 2-2: A pre-lobby News screen on the Nintendo Switch.

From this News screen, you can go directly to the lobby, select the Item Shop to make cosmetics purchases, or view the patch notes, which detail what has changed with the latest version of the game. This News screen and its options are also available from the lobby.

Getting to Know the Lobby

The lobby, shown in Figure 2-3, appears after selecting the option from the News screen. This extensive series of menus, with your character at the center, is your hub for selecting game options, adding friends, joining parties, tracking weekly and daily challenges, and everything else you will need access to before playing Fortnite. This is also the screen you'll return to after the end of a match.

FIGURE 2-3: The lobby on the PlayStation 4.

The best way to learn all the functions and features is to move around the lobby menu and select things. Nothing much happens until you select Play in the lower-right corner, which locks in all of the settings you chose and begins the selected game type.

Although there are slight differences with Fortnite's lobby setup between different platforms, you should familiarize yourself with the following major components, as highlighted in Figure 2-4:

>> **Friends:** Found in the upper left of the lobby, this shows the number of your Epic Games friends currently online. Selecting this option brings up the My Friends and Add Friends tab menus.

>> **Menu Options:** Found in the upper center of the lobby. Besides Lobby, there are the following options:

- *Battle Pass:* Purchase or manage the current season's Battle Pass.

- *Challenges:* Grouped by Event, Daily, Weekly, and Style.

- *Events:* Review past, current, and future events.

- *Locker:* Manage your current gear and outfits.

- *Item Shop:* Use V-Bucks to purchase various cosmetics.

- *Career:* Look at your career profile in all Battle Royale modes, as well as view various leaderboards with ranked player scores, places, and wins.
- *Store:* Purchase various V-Bucks bundles.

>> **V-Bucks:** Found in the upper right, just before Settings. Shows how many V-Bucks you have left to spend.

>> **Settings:** Found in the upper right, just after V-Bucks. This is where you can tweak your graphic and sound preferences, customize your controls, manage multiplayer settings, and more. See the next section for details.

>> **Data Center:** Found in the upper right, just below V-Bucks and Settings. Shows the current server region you're connected to for the lowest in-game ping rate. You'll typically be auto-routed to the most optimal region, but, should you have to, you can manually set the region under Settings.

Squad Slot
Datacenter
Season   Settings
Friends   Menu Options   V-Bucks

Challenges   Your Character   Info Buttons   Play
Pass Tier   Match Type

FIGURE 2-4: The lobby on the PlayStation 4 with highlighted sections.

Ping is the network latency, measured in milliseconds (ms), between computers used in online gaming. A high ping of over 100 ms can result in high latency, causing a lag between actions and what is happening on screen.

>> **Season:** Found in the upper left below Friends. Shows your season level, how much experience (XP) you have, and how much you need to reach the next level. At the start of each new season, your level progression resets.

>> **Pass Tier:** Found in the left below Season and above Challenges. Indicates your current tier on either the Free Pass or Battle Pass. Gaining stars unlocks rewards. You advance a tier for every 10 stars earned.

>> **Challenges:** Found in the left below Pass Tier. This can be cycled between Suggested Challenges, which are daily or weekly challenges to meet one or more times, and Party Assist Challenges, where you can work with others to beat challenges you are stuck on.

>> **Your Character:** Found in the center of the screen. This is your current character, and it shows exactly how you will look in the game.

>> **Squad Slot:** Found to the left and right of your character. Besides your character, there are three other Squad Slots for each of the team members in a Squads mode game. You simply select an empty Squad Slot to invite a friend from your Epic Games friend list. After they accept, their character will appear in the slot.

>> **Match Type:** Found in the lower right of the screen above Play. This shows the actively selected game mode. Select it to change between the various Solo, Duos, Squads, and Creative game types.

>> **Play:** Found in the lower right of the screen, below Match Type and above the Info Buttons. Select this button to go to Spawn Island. This is a pre-game meeting area where you're free to shoot, build, loot, and otherwise practice before the Battle Bus comes and takes you to the battlefield.

>> **Info Buttons:** Found on the bottom of the screen. Indicates what to press, respectively, to voice chat, cycle through the Challenges, select an Emote to see your character perform, or see the News screen. These functions can be reconfigured under Settings.

Adjusting Settings

The Settings menu is found in the upper right of the lobby, as shown in Figure 2-4. When you select this option, you'll see a screen similar to the one in Figure 2-5.

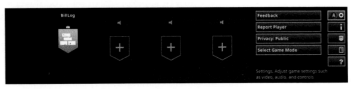

FIGURE 2-5: Fortnite Settings screen on Xbox One.

Most of what's on this screen is informational, save for the gear icon in the upper right that's the main way to modify various settings and controls. The left side of this menu shows your character's banner and the three slots for potential squad members. For everything else, here are brief descriptions:

>> **Feedback:** Send feedback via a form about bugs or game experiences.

>> **Report Player:** Report another player for a communication abuse, offensive name, teaming up with enemies, harassment, or cheating and hacking.

>> **Privacy:** Change your privacy setting to allow others to join your game. The possible options are Public, Friends, or Private.

>> **Select Game Mode:** Return to the Game Mode selection screen.

>> **i icon:** Fortnite legal information, which includes the End User License Agreement, or EULA, and the Third Party Software Notice.

>> **Epic Games icon:** Fortnite's design, development, and publishing credits.

>> **Clipboard icon:** Opens the epicgames.com website and shows the latest code of conduct requirements.

>> **Question Mark icon:** Opens the epicgames.helpshift.com website and provides links to know more about various topics related to Epic Games and Fortnite.

Below the question mark on the PC and Mac versions of Fortnite, there's an Exit the Game button. For all other platforms, you quit the game like you would any other game or app. Some platforms also have a log out icon, which logs you out of your current account login and looks like a door frame with a left pointing arrow in the middle.

On the iOS and Android versions, there are two additional options, Controls Help and HUD layout tool. Controls Help shows an annotated picture of both the in-game Combat mode and Build mode controls, whereas the HUD layout tool lets you move various onscreen elements for the standard heads up display to suit your personal preferences.

When clicking on the gear icon in the upper right of the Settings screen, you're presented with tab options similar to those shown in Figure 2-6. From left to right, the tab options are:

>> **Video:** The first icon, showing a monitor, and which is not available on Nintendo Switch. Adjusts various visual settings to either improve the look or performance of the game.

>> **Game:** The second icon, showing gears. Adjusts region and various input settings.

>> **Brightness:** The sun icon, not available on iOS or Android. Adjusts the display's brightness.

>> **Audio:** The speaker icon. Adjusts volume and other sound-related settings.

>> **Accessibility:** The person icon, not available on iOS or Android. Adds or modifies adjustments to aid those with visual or hearing impairments.

>> **Input:** The cursor keys icon, only available on PC, Mac, PlayStation 4, or Xbox One. Adjusts assigned keyboard and mouse control actions.

>> **Controller:** The gamepad icon. Configures assigned combat and building controls when using a gamepad.

>> **Account:** The torso icon. Shows your Epic Account ID and lets you configure privacy and social settings.

The subsections that follow detail the tabs under Settings. Most tab options have a tooltip or other descriptive text to help you understand what a particular function or setting does.

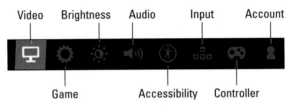

Video   Brightness   Audio   Input   Account

Game   Accessibility   Controller

FIGURE 2-6: PC Settings options.

TIP

Don't be afraid to make changes to various settings once you become more comfortable with the game. You can always select Reset to reset the tab options back to their defaults.

Video tab

The Video tab, whose PC version is shown in Figure 2-7, is automatically configured to give you the best performance on your specific system. Although the Video menu is limited to turning Motion Blur on or off on Xbox One and PlayStation 4 (and is not present at all on Nintendo Switch), you can use this menu to tweak the look and performance of your game on PC, Mac, iOS, and Android. Generally speaking, lowering or turning off a setting results in a performance improvement. When it comes to a battery powered device, lowering or turning off settings should help increase battery life as well.

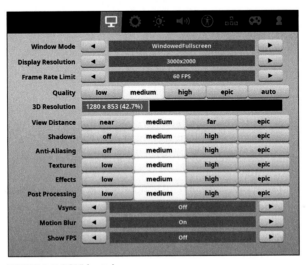

FIGURE 2-7: PC Video tab.

Game tab

The Game tab, whose PC version is shown in Figure 2-8, is divided into sections as follows:

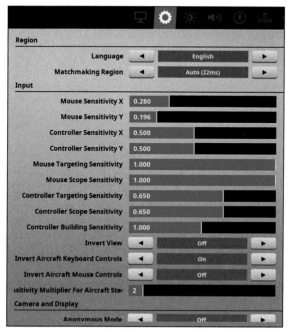

FIGURE 2-8: PC Game tab.

The major sections are described as follows:

>> **Region:** Under Language, you can set the language you want to display for all in-game text. Under Matchmaking Region, you set which Epic Games server you will connect to. In most instances, leaving this set to Auto gives you optimal results, but you can scroll through the options to see whether your ping time is improved by switching servers manually.

>> **Input:** This contains various options to set mouse, controller, touch, or motion sensitivity. You can also invert many of the controls, for instance, in order to look down when you push the controller up and vice-versa.

» **Camera and Display:** This section is available on all but iOS and Android, whose relevant features are rolled into Input. These settings let you choose whether your name appears to other players, whether to hide other players' names, and other features that affect in-game information displays.

» **Control Options:** This area sets how you play and react during a match. Many of these features are particularly useful, so are worth describing in a bit more detail:

- *Toggle Sprint:* Sets sprint to be an on/off toggle or a hold to sprint. When on, sprint is set to an on/off toggle with one press.

- *Sprint by Default:* When on, you automatically sprint when moving and the sprint control will make you walk.

- *Sprint Cancels Reloading:* When on, you stop reloading a weapon and sprint when sprinting is engaged.

- *Tap to Search/Interact:* When on, Search/Interact requires a single press. When off, the control must be held for the duration of the timer.

- *Toggle Targeting:* When on, the targeting control is an on/off toggle. When off, the targeting control is a hold.

- *Reset Building Choice:* When on, switching to Build mode always brings up the first build piece. When off, the game remembers to bring up the last build piece you were using.

- *Aim Assist:* When on, attracts your aim towards enemy players when using a gamepad.

- *Edit Mode Aim Assist:* When on, attracts your aim towards the closest editing square when building in Edit mode using a gamepad.

- *Turbo Building:* When on, holding down the Build button automatically continues to build the selected piece when looking around. When off, each build requires one press or click.

- *Turbo Delete in Creative Mode:* When on, enables the ability to rapidly delete things in Creative mode by holding down the Delete button.

- *Auto Material Change:* When on, you automatically swap to a new material type when you try to build but do not have enough of the currently selected material.

- *Controller Auto-Run:* When on, double-clicking the movement stick makes you automatically run forward without needing to hold the stick forward.

- *Auto Open Doors:* When on, doors automatically open when you approach them.

- *Auto Pick Up Weapons:* When on, weapons are automatically picked up when you move over them, unless your inventory is full.

- *Auto Sort Consumables to Right:* When on, consumables such as health and shields default to the rightmost empty Quickbar slot when picked up.

- *Builder Pro: Build Immediately:* When on, when switching to a different build piece using Builder Pro, it will try to build immediately.

- *Controller Edit Hold Time:* Sets the duration to hold the button down for entering Edit mode.

» **Feedback:** Sets controller vibration on or off. On select hardware, you can also set other feedback-related features on or off, as well as the Power Saving option.

» **Replays:** PC, Mac, PlayStation 4, and Xbox One owners can turn on replay recording, which records and stores replays after each match. However, recording replays can reduce performance and take up storage space, so use it wisely.

Brightness tab

The Brightness tab, whose PC version is shown in Figure 2-9, lets you adjust the brightness of your display. If you play in a darker room, you'll want to lower the brightness setting. In a lighter room, you'll want to raise the brightness setting.

Audio tab

The Audio tab, whose PC version is shown in Figure 2-10, lets you individually adjust music, sound effects, voice chat, and cinematics volume. You can also turn subtitles on or off and adjust voice chat and related settings.

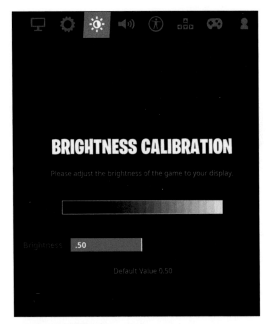

FIGURE 2-9: PC Brightness tab.

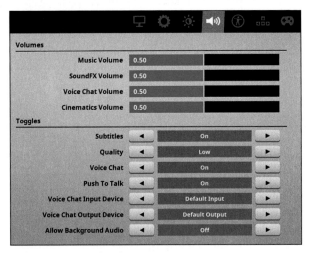

FIGURE 2-10: PC Audio tab.

Accessibility tab

The Accessibility tab, whose PC version is shown in Figure 2-11, lets you set Color Blind mode, accommodate input when using accessible controls, or visualize sound effects.

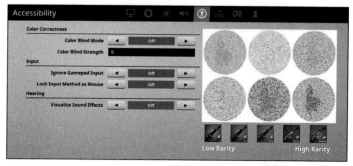

FIGURE 2-11: PC Accessibility tab.

Input tab

The Input tab, whose PC version is shown in Figure 2-12, lets you adjust keyboard and mouse function mapping. This tab is available full-time on PC and Mac. PlayStation 4 and Xbox One players have access to this tab only if they connect a keyboard and mouse to their consoles.

Controller tab

The Controller tab, whose PC version is shown in Figure 2-13, lets you choose between a selection of custom combat and build controls, as well as adjust the analog sensitivity of your gamepad. You can also choose a custom configuration and assign controls and buttons to almost any function you'd like. On the PC and Mac, you can also select between PlayStation 4 and Xbox One controller standards based on the type of gamepad you use.

Account tab

The Account tab, whose PC version is shown in Figure 2-14, is divided into Account Info, Content, and Social functions. Of particular note is the Content area, in which you can request a refund for non-consumable purchases, although you get only three total such requests for the lifetime of your account.

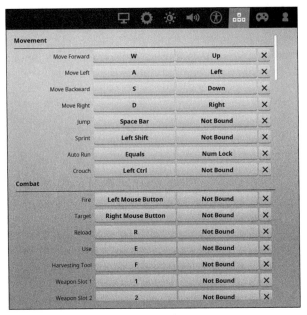

FIGURE 2-12: PC Input tab.

FIGURE 2-13: PC Controller tab.

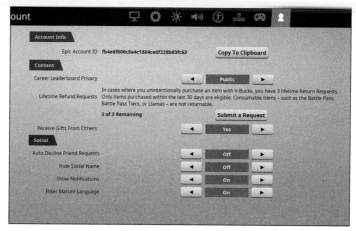

FIGURE 2-14: PC Account tab.

Getting to Know the Controls

As you can see, Fortnite is a complex game with incredible depth. For better or worse, that depth carries over to the game's controls. Whether you're sporting a keyboard and mouse, a gamepad, or a touchscreen, you'll need to master the game's controls. The subsections that follow provide a handy reference for the default control setups.

TIP

It's strongly recommended that you master one of the default control schemes before using a custom profile or assigning actions to new keys or buttons. You'll likely need to play quite a few Battle Royale rounds before you gain enough experience to evaluate your play style and what changes might make the most sense.

Understanding the fundamentals

A basic sequence of Fortnite controls apply regardless of how you're controlling the game. Let's review these core gameplay mechanics:

>> **Movement:** You need to walk or sprint, jump, and crouch. You'll also need to separately move the camera to look around.

>> **Combat:** To fight, aim your weapon and then fire, or look down the sights and aim, then fire.

Although reloading your weapon is automatic, manual reloads are recommended when you're low on ammo so you're at full strength quicker. Always look for ways to save time in-game. Seconds count!

>> **Inventory:** You need to pick items up and then toggle between the items in your six inventory slots to use them. You can also reorder items in your inventory, moving them between the different slots.

>> **Building:** Harvest items by hitting them with your pickaxe. When ready to build, manually switch to Build mode. From there, you can swap materials, place items, and then edit them. When you run out of a material, the game automatically switches to the next one, or you can switch manually. When finished building, be sure to switch back to Combat mode.

Because building is critical for both good offensive and defensive battle strategies, the faster you can switch between Build and Combat modes, the more effective fighter you'll be!

Using a keyboard and mouse

You can use a keyboard and mouse on a PC, Mac, PlayStation 4, or Xbox One in Input mode. Input control categories are broken into Movement, Combat, Building, Communication, Emote, Misc, Vehicles, and Creative, as described in the following subsections.

Movement

The default input controls for movement are shown in Table 2-1.

Combat

The default input controls for combat are shown in Table 2-2.

Building

The default input controls for building are shown in Table 2-3.

Communication

The default input controls for communication are shown in Table 2-4.

TABLE 2-1 Input Controls for Movement

Action	Keyboard Key	Mouse Action
Move forward	W	Up
Move left	A	Left
Move backward	S	Down
Move right	D	Right
Jump	Spacebar	Not assigned
Sprint	Left Shift	Not assigned
Auto run	Equals	Num Lock
Crouch	Left Ctrl	Not assigned

TABLE 2-2 Input Controls for Combat

Action	Keyboard Key	Mouse Action
Fire	None	Left mouse button
Target	None	Right mouse button
Reload	R	Not assigned
Use	E	Not assigned
Harvesting tool	F	Not assigned
Weapon slot 1	1	Not assigned
Weapon slot 2	2	Not assigned
Weapon slot 3	3	Not assigned
Weapon slot 4	4	Not assigned
Weapon slot 5	5	Not assigned

TABLE 2-3 **Input Controls for Building**

Action	Keyboard Key	Mouse Action
Crouch while building	Left Ctrl	Not assigned
Wall	Z	Thumb mouse button 2
Floor	X	Not assigned
Stairs	C	Thumb mouse button
Roof	V	Not assigned
Trap	V	Not assigned
Place building	Not assigned	Left mouse button
Repair/upgrade	H	Not assigned
Rotate building	R	Not assigned
Change building material	None	Right mouse button
Crouch while editing	Left Ctrl	Not assigned
Select building edit	Not assigned	Left mouse button
Reset building edit	Not assigned	Right mouse button

TABLE 2-4 **Input Controls for Communication**

Action	Keyboard Key	Mouse Action
Ping/place marker	Not assigned	Middle mouse button
Place enemy marker	Not assigned	Not assigned
Push to talk	T	Not assigned
Squad comms	F4	Not assigned
Chat	Enter	Not assigned

Emote

The default input controls for emote are shown in Table 2-5.

Misc

The default input controls for misc are shown in Table 2-6.

TABLE 2-5 **Input Controls for Emote**

Action	Keyboard Key	Mouse Action
Emote	B	Not assigned
Locker emote slot 1	Not assigned	Not assigned
Locker emote slot 2	Not assigned	Not assigned
Locker emote slot 3	Not assigned	Not assigned
Locker emote slot 4	Not assigned	Not assigned
Locker emote slot 5	Not assigned	Not assigned
Locker emote slot 6	Not assigned	Not assigned
Repeat last emote	Not assigned	Not assigned

TABLE 2-6 **Input Controls for Misc**

Action	Keyboard Key	Mouse Action
Building edit	G	Not assigned
Toggle harvesting tool	L	Not assigned
Trap equip/picker	F3	Not assigned
Switch Quickbar	Q	Not assigned
Slot up	Mouse wheel down	Not assigned
Slot down	Mouse wheel up	Not assigned
Previous picker wheel	Mouse wheel down	Not assigned
Next picker wheel	Mouse wheel up	Not assigned
Cursor mode	Left Alt/Right Alt	Not assigned
Toggle map	M	Not assigned
Toggle inventory	Tab/I	Not assigned

Vehicles

The default input controls for vehicles are shown in Table 2-7.

Creative

The default input controls for Creative mode are shown in Table 2-8.

TABLE 2-7 **Input Controls for Vehicles**

Action	Keyboard Key	Mouse Action
Vehicle exit	E	Not assigned
Vehicle change seat	Left Ctrl	Not assigned
Vehicle honk horn	Not assigned	Right mouse button
Vehicle pitch forward	S	Down
Vehicle pitch backward	W	Up
Shopping cart — Push (tap)/ coast (hold)	Space bar	Not assigned
Pirate cannon — Fire	Not assigned	Left mouse button
Pirate cannon — Fire (2)	Not assigned	Not assigned
Pirate cannon — Push (tap)/ coast (hold)	Space bar	Not assigned
Pirate cannon — Push (tap)/ coast (hold) (2)	Space bar	Not assigned
All terrain kart (ATK) powerslide	Space bar	Not assigned
Quadcrasher boost	Space bar	Not assigned
Driftboard boost	Left Shift	Not assigned
Driftboard use/exit	E	Not assigned
Baller boost	Space bar	Not assigned
Baller shoot/contract grapple	Not assigned	Left mouse button
Baller extend grapple	Not assigned	Right mouse button
Biplane boost	Space bar	Not assigned
Biplane shoot	Left mouse button	Not assigned
Biplane roll right	C	Not assigned
Biplane roll left	Z	Not assigned
Biplane roll invert	X	Not assigned
Biplane start engine	W/Space bar	Not assigned
Biplane stop engine	Left Shift	Not assigned
Biplane free look	Not assigned	Right mouse button

TABLE 2-8 **Input Controls for Creative**

Action	Keyboard Key	Mouse Action
Creative pick up/exit	Not assigned	Right mouse button
Creative copy	Not assigned	Left mouse button
Creative delete	X	Not assigned
Creative prop copy	Not assigned	Left mouse button
Creative prop toggle drop	G	Not assigned
Creative prop rotate clockwise	R	Not assigned
Creative prop rotate counterclockwise	E	Not assigned
Creative prop rotation axis (tap)/ reset (hold)	Tab	Not assigned
Creative prop push	F	Not assigned
Creative prop pull	C	Not assigned
Creative prop exit	Escape	Right mouse button
Creative prop grid Snap	V	Not assigned
Creative building copy	Not assigned	Left mouse button
Creative building rotate clockwise	R	Not assigned
Creative building rotate counterclockwise	Z	Not assigned
Creative building mirror	M	Not assigned
Creative building exit	Escape	Right mouse button
Creative building grid snap	V	Not assigned
Creative fly up	Left Shift	Not assigned
Creative fly down	Left Ctrl	Not assigned
Creative island panel support creator	Q	Not assigned
Creative island panel start game	E	Not assigned

Using a gamepad

Gamepads, or game controllers, work on every platform, including iOS and Android. For PlayStation 4, Xbox One, and Nintendo Switch, gamepad controls are designed around their standard controller layouts. PC and Macintosh users can choose between Xbox One and PlayStation 4 layouts, depending upon which controller type they use with their systems. Most MFi controllers for iOS devices and Android-compatible Bluetooth controllers tend to use the Xbox One controller's layout.

There are five different controller configurations, each designed to optimize the layout for a particular play style: Old School, Quick Builder, Combat Pro, Builder Pro, and Custom, as well as specific combat controls and build controls for each. Builder Pro is what Fortnite defaults to, and it has proven to be the most popular configuration. Those controls are shown in Table 2-9 and Table 2-10. Table 2-9 shows the combat controls.

TABLE 2-9 **Builder Pro for Combat Controls for Xbox One, PlayStation 4, and Nintendo Switch**

Action	Xbox One	PlayStation 4	Nintendo Switch
Aim down sights	Left trigger	L2	ZL
Previous weapon	Left bumper	L1	L
Move	Left stick	Left stick	Left stick
Sprint/auto-sprint (double-click)	Left stick click	Left stick click	Left stick click
Inventory (management, etc.)	Directional pad up	Directional button up	Directional button up
Emote	Directional pad down	Directional button down	Directional button down
Place marker	Directional pad left	Direction button left	Directional button left
Squad comms	Directional pad right	Directional button right	Directional button right
Game menu (friends, etc.)	Menu button	SHARE button	Plus button
Toggle map	View button	Touch pad button	Minus button

Action	Xbox One	PlayStation 4	Nintendo Switch
Attack/confirm	Right trigger	R2	ZR
Next weapon	Right bumper	R1	R
Toggle harvesting tool	Y button	Triangle button	X
Reload/interact (tap/hold)	X button	Square button	Y button
Toggle Build mode/ edit building piece (hold)	B button	Circle button	A button
Jump	A button	X Button	B button
Look	Right stick	Right stick	Right stick
Crouch (tap)/ repair (hold)	Right stick click	Right stick click	Rick stick click

Table 2-10 shows the build controls.

TABLE 2-10 **Builder Pro for Build Controls for Xbox One, PlayStation 4, and Nintendo Switch**

Action	Xbox One	PlayStation 4	Nintendo Switch
Stair piece (tap select/tap place)	Left trigger	L2	ZL
Roof piece (tap select/tap place)	Left bumper	L1	L
Move	Left stick	Left stick	Left stick
Sprint/auto-sprint (double-click)	Left stick click	Left stick click	Left stick click
Inventory (management, etc.)	Directional pad up	Directional button up	Directional button up
Emote	Directional pad down	Directional button down	Directional button down
Change building material/trap	Directional pad left	Direction button left	Directional button left

(continued)

TABLE 2-10 *(continued)*

Action	Xbox One	PlayStation 4	Nintendo Switch
Squad comms	Directional pad right	Directional button right	Directional button right
Game menu (friends, etc.)	Menu button	SHARE button	Plus button
Toggle map	View button	Touch pad button	Minus button
Wall piece (tap select/tap place)	Right trigger	R2	ZR
Floor piece (tap select/tap place)	Right bumper	R1	R
Toggle harvesting tool	Y button	Triangle button	X
Trap (tap select/ tap place)/interact (tap/hold)	X button	Square button	Y button
Toggle Build mode/edit building piece (hold)	B button	Circle button	A button
Jump	A button	X button	B button
Look	Right stick	Right stick	Right stick
Rotate building piece (tap)/repair (hold)/change trapt/reset building edit (Edit mode)	Right stick click	Right stick click	Right stick click

Using a touchscreen

Although iOS and Android users can utilize a gamepad, the most common control option is your mobile device's built-in touchscreen. Figure 2-15 shows the basic default combat controls for touchscreens.

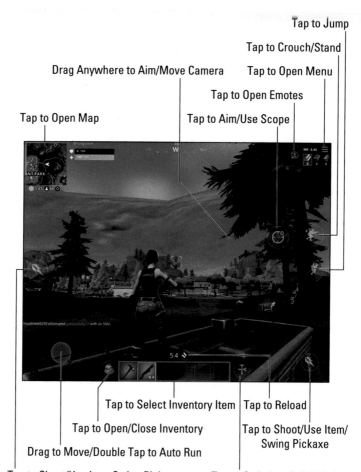

Tap to Jump

Tap to Crouch/Stand

Drag Anywhere to Aim/Move Camera   Tap to Open Menu

Tap to Open Emotes

Tap to Open Map   Tap to Aim/Use Scope

Tap to Select Inventory Item | Tap to Reload

Tap to Open/Close Inventory   Tap to Shoot/Use Item/
Swing Pickaxe

Drag to Move/Double Tap to Auto Run

Tap to Shoot/Use Item Swing Pickaxe   Tap to Switch to Build Mode

FIGURE 2-15: Default combat control HUD for touchscreens (iPad screen shown).

REMEMBER

The HUD Layout tool, found under Settings, lets you move various onscreen elements for the standard heads-up display to suit your personal preferences. As with modifying keyboard and mouse and gamepad controls, it's best to leave the screen layout in its default configuration until you get more comfortable with the game.

Figure 2-16 shows the basic default build controls for touchscreens.

Tap to Jump

Rotate Structure

Drag Anywhere to Aim/Move Camera   Tap to Open Menu

Tap to Open Emotes

Tap to Open Map   Edit Structure

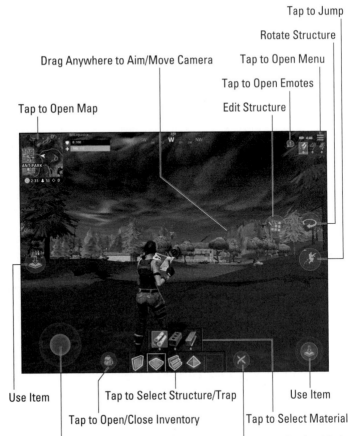

Use Item   Tap to Select Structure/Trap   Use Item

Tap to Open/Close Inventory   Tap to Select Material

Drag to Move/Double Tap to Auto Run   Tap to Switch to Combat Mode

FIGURE 2-16: Default build control HUD for touchscreens (iPad screen shown).

Buying Accessories

To play Fortnite, all you really need is one of the supported platforms with standard controls and a good Internet connection. Of course, just playing a game and playing a game in an optimal way are two different things.

There's the obvious, like a faster, more powerful computer with a discrete, high-end graphics card, the latest and greatest versions of a console or mobile device, and the fastest, biggest display married to the best sound system. You can, however, improve your overall experience for a lot less with accessories like a better mouse, keyboard, gamepad, or headset.

Here are some things to look out for when purchasing accessories to improve not only your Fortnite experience but also your experience with other games and the overall enjoyment of your system of choice:

>> **Mice:** A good mouse for Fortnite is one that allows you to move quickly and precisely, and also has at least a few extra buttons you can program for some of the "not assigned" functions in Tables 2-1 through 2-8. Keep an eye out for mice that are designed for gaming, like the high resolution and physically configurable Razer DeathAdder Elite ($69.99) or Corsair Glaive RGB gaming mouse ($69.99), shown in Figure 2-17. Although pro gamers tend to prefer wired mice to minimize input delays or signal interference, the Logitech G Pro Wireless ($149.99) uses proprietary wireless technology to match or exceed the performance of its wired competitors.

Source: Amazon.com

FIGURE 2-17: The Corsair Glaive RGB gaming mouse features interchangeable thumb grips for a more customized feel.

» **Keyboards:** Keyboards that come with computers are usually low on features and performance. Gaming keyboards, on the other hand, typically have a host of programmable keys and mechanical switches that have a satisfying feel and quicker key response rate. Keyboards like the Corsair K95 RGB Platinum ($159.99), which features Cherry MX Speed keyswitches on an aluminum frame with customizable profile storage, or the HyperX Alloy Elite RGB ($139.99), shown in Figure 2-18, with a choice of keyswitches and customizable software of its own, are two excellent examples.

FIGURE 2-18: The HyperX Alloy Elite RGB comes with optional textured keys to replace the usual W, A, S, and D movement keys and the first four function keys.

» **Gamepads:** Although the standard gamepads for the PlayStation 4, Xbox One, and Nintendo Switch definitely get the job done, there are some better options out there. For PlayStation 4, there are controllers like the Razer Raiju Pro gaming controller ($149.99), which features instant controller customization and more responsive triggers and buttons. For Xbox One, there are controllers like the Microsoft Xbox

Elite wireless controller ($149.99), shown in Figure 2-19, which has a premium feel and swappable components. For Nintendo Switch, one of the best alternatives to the standard Joy-Cons is Nintendo's own Nintendo Switch Pro controller ($69.99), which is a comfortable dedicated gamepad with motion controls, HD rumble, and built-in Amiibo functionality.

FIGURE 2-19: The Microsoft Xbox Elite wireless controller comes with four sets of paddles, six thumbsticks, and two D-pads, so you can mix and match parts to find the perfect fit.

>> **Headsets:** A good gaming headset not only allows you to clearly hear all of the in-game sound effects, including the all-important direction you're being shot from, but, thanks to a built-in microphone, also lets you talk to your teammates to better coordinate your actions. Although it's tough to find gaming headsets that work with every platform, some examples include the Kingston HyperX Cloud Stinger gaming headset ($49.99), which plugs into any standard headphone

jack, and the high-end Victrix Pro AF universal wired gaming headset with active noise cancellation ($299.99), shown in Figure 2-20. Of course, if you'd like a platform-specific headset, there are plenty of great wired and wireless options out there, many with superb surround sound and comfortable and breathable earpads for those long and intense play sessions.

Source: Amazon.com

FIGURE 2-20: The Victrix Pro AF universal wired gaming headset with active noise cancellation reduces up to 70 percent of background noise, so you can really focus on what you're playing.

IN THIS CHAPTER

» Understanding how play unfolds

» Knowing when to jump and where to land

» Searching for and gathering loot

» Staying ahead of the storm

» Surviving on your own

» Playing with others

Chapter **3**

Playing Your First Games

N ow that you have a sense of how Fortnite works from Chapter 1 and how to customize what you need to from Chapter 2, it's time to play your first Battle Royale games. Regardless of whether you choose a Solo, Duos, or Squads game type, the overarching structure remains the same.

Understanding the Sequence of Play

A Battle Royale game consists of four major sequences before a victor is declared. Let's review this progression:

» **Pre-deployment zone:** After you select a Solo, Duos, or Squads game type, you'll be transported to the pre-deployment zone. This is the post-lobby waiting area where you can practice consequence-free until all other players join the game.

» **Battle Bus:** After all the players are in place, you'll automatically be transported aboard the flying Battle Bus, which takes a random route across the island. Because the Battle Bus never lands, you need to choose when to leap from the bus and freefall towards land. Deploy the glider to slow your descent and fine tune your landing spot.

TIP

If you forget to jump from the Battle Bus or deploy the glider, the game will automatically take over to complete either action at the last moment as needed. These are the only times the game will help you out, so be sure to stay focused!

>> **On the ground:** After landing, you only have your pickaxe, so your first order of business is to try and find a weapon. As you search for a weapon, take time along the way to gather materials with your pickaxe. Loot away!

>> **Battle:** The remaining part of the game is devoted to putting yourself in the best offensive and defensive positions. Even if you try and avoid conflicts, the approaching storm circle eventually makes the safe zone play area too small. No matter what, you'll eventually be forced to fight!

You'll need to master the various building techniques, weapons, and other items to overcome your enemies. Don't worry if you or your team keep getting smoked in the beginning. Practice makes perfect, or at least better, so keep at it!

Practicing in the Pre-Deployment Area

The pre-deployment area, shown in Figure 3-1, is your one place to practice just about anything you'd like before being placed under the intense pressure of both your opponents and the encroaching storm circle. Many players use this brief time before all players are present and being sent to the Battle Bus to find weapons and practice all that goes into their effective usage like aiming, shooting, reloading, and switching between the other items in your inventory. Of course, you can also practice other in-game actions, like building basic forts, which can prove almost as important as skillful use of your weapons.

If you're already comfortable with the controls, you can instead use your time in the pre-deployment area to press the Map button. When displaying the map, you'll see the random route the Battle Bus will take and can plan where you might want to jump. By planning in advance, you won't have to worry about figuring out when to jump on the moving Battle Bus and possibly miss out on an ideal landing spot.

FIGURE 3-1: The pre-deployment area lets you practice just about anything you'd like before automatically boarding the Battle Bus.

Knowing When to Jump

After spending some time in the pre-deployment area, you're automatically taken to the flying Battle Bus, as shown in Figure 3-2, where you're joined by up to 99 other players. Although the island itself generally remains the same within a particular season, each match randomizes the island's safe zones and loot chest locations, as well as the path the bus takes.

Although the bus path is different every time, it always goes in a straight line. If you haven't jumped off before the bus reaches the end of its route and time runs out, you'll be automatically pushed off.

TIP

You may have noticed the "*playername* has thanked the bus driver" messages on the lower left of the screen. If you too want to thank the bus driver, you can do so by pressing down on the D-pad (Xbox One/PlayStation 4/Nintendo Switch), pressing the B key (PC/Mac), or pressing the emote icon on the right side of the screen (mobile) before jumping off the Battle Bus. For now, it makes absolutely no difference to the gameplay, but it's still a fun, quirky action not every player knows how to do.

FIGURE 3-2: Aboard the Battle Bus.

Knowing Where to Land

Although you can jump off the Battle Bus at any time, having a strategy in place before leaping gives you a better chance of surviving early battles. Whereas Chapter 4 provides a detailed look at the map and some pluses and minuses for various locations, you'll still need to know how to get to where you want to go once you're in the game. That's where a map marker comes in.

When displaying the map, you can set a map marker that leaves a blue diamond on the map display, like in Figure 3-3. This blue diamond shows up as a long blue flare on the ground after you leave the Battle Bus, as in Figure 3-4. Because you have limited control over your freefall, you want to time your jump off the Battle Bus so you're within a reasonable distance of your intended target.

When in freefall, you can increase your descent speed by pointing down. You can also manually deploy your glider to both slow your descent and have better control over the direction you're falling. The quicker you can land, however, the better, because this gives you more time to loot and find much-needed weapons and supplies.

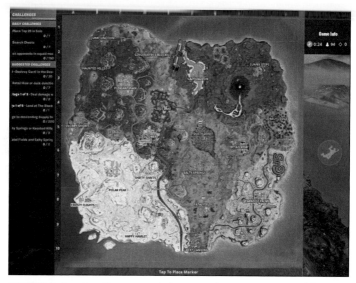

FIGURE 3-3: Summon the map and place a marker as soon as possible so you can properly time your jump off the Battle Bus.

The game automatically deploys your glider when you're close to the ground and keeps it deployed until you've landed, so feel free to be as aggressive as possible with your descent.

FIGURE 3-4: Direct your freefall towards the marker you set, which is represented in-game as a blue flare.

Searching for and Gathering Loot

Because guns beat pickaxes every time, when you're on the ground, you have to quickly start looting. You'll obviously be slow to do things when you first start playing, but once you get the hang of the admittedly dense control system, your next order of business is to learn to perform each action as quickly as possible. Speed usually wins out above all else in Fortnite, and gathering materials as quickly as possible goes a long way towards success.

You have six inventory slots, but the first slot always has your pickaxe, as shown in Figure 3-5. That leaves five other slots for weapons and healing items. As soon as you're on the ground, locate at least one weapon. Search everywhere, including inside, behind, and on top of buildings and vehicles. Locate and smash crates and open chests for even more loot!

FIGURE 3-5: The pickaxe and the remaining five inventory slots are found in the lower right of your screen. Fill those empty slots fast to have the best chance at survival, but always be ready to replace existing inventory with something better!

TIP

Try to be consistent with where you place weapons like grenades and other items like medical packs in your five inventory slots. Knowing that a particular item is always in the same spot can help leverage your muscle memory when seconds count.

When you have a weapon, use your pickaxe to gather materials from houses, trees, vehicles, and other items. Nearly everything is destructible. Alternate between searching for weapons and other items like shield potions and gathering materials with which to build structures like forts and bridges.

You can hold unlimited ammunition, so always pick it up whenever you come across it.

Staying Ahead of the Storm

Along with everything else you have to manage and deal with in Fortnite's Battle Royale, there's also an ever-present storm. This deadly storm not only reduces visibility when you're caught in it, but also damages your health. If you don't stay ahead of the storm and stay in its eye, the safe zone, you will get hurt and maybe even die. The safe zone is the shape of a circle centered somewhere on the map, as shown in Figure 3-6.

FIGURE 3-6: The storm's eye, or safe zone, is represented by a circle on the map. Stay within the circle to avoid taking damage.

As the safe zone continues to shrink, you'll need to keep moving. Eventually, the storm itself moves, so you'll have to keep moving with it to stay in the ever-shrinking safe zone.

Other players will be trying to stay safe from the storm as well, so as the storm circle decreases, expect more frequent battles. Be ready on both offense and defense!

The blue timer icon, which is shown in Figure 3-7, appears just below the mini map or to the right of the full screen map; it shows how much time is left before the next storm event. When the safe zone starts shrinking or moving, the blue timer icon changes to a flashing pink storm cloud icon. This flashing pink storm cloud icon changes back to a blue timer icon when the event stops.

Timer

FIGURE 3-7: The storm timer.

In the early stages of a match, the storm simply shrinks. In the later stages of a match, the storm both shrinks and moves. As with increased shrinking and movement, damage to your health goes from one point per second all the way up to ten points per second as the match progresses. Table 3-1 provides a handy table of storm activity that's current as of this writing. Plan your strategy accordingly!

TABLE 3-1 **Storm Event Timing and Damage**

Storm Phase	Event Timing	Shrink Timing	Damage Inside Storm
Circle 1	3 minutes, 20 seconds	3 minutes	1 point per second
Circle 2	2 minutes	2 minutes	1 point per second
Circle 3	1 minute, 30 seconds	1 minute, 30 seconds	2 points per second
Circle 4	1 minute, 20 seconds	1 minute, 10 seconds	5 points per second
Circle 5 — Moving	50 seconds	60 seconds	10 points per second
Circle 6 — Moving	30 seconds	60 seconds	10 points per second
Circle 7 — Moving	No wait	55 seconds	10 points per second
Circle 8 — Moving	No wait	45 seconds	10 points per second
Circle 9 — Moving	No wait	75 seconds	10 points per second

Surviving on Your Own

It's every person for themselves! To survive on your own in a Solo mode, you'll need to do everything possible to put yourself in the best offensive and defensive positions. However, even if you do everything right, there's still a good chance you'll die. A lot. Even the best players tend to lose more often than they win. Fortnite is a game that relies on creativity and luck almost as much as it does on skill, so don't be too bummed if you keep on losing. Take solace in the fact that there's always another match ready and waiting, and next time just might be the time it all comes together for you. Even if it doesn't, though, you will still have a blast trying.

An interesting feature of Fortnite is that after you're eliminated from a match, the game switches to the perspective of the person who killed you. If that person is eliminated, it switches viewpoints to their killer. Although you may be tempted to exit the game, return to the lobby, and try again, it's actually beneficial to stick around once in a while and watch how others play. You can not only learn new strategies and techniques, but can also get a better sense of the island's geography and landmarks. After all, it's hard to pay attention to your surroundings when you're trying to fight off other players and keep track of the storm circle.

Playing with Other Players

Although you can go it alone, Fortnite is at its best when played with friends or other teammates. By teaming up, your chances of winning go up dramatically, particularly if you're not yet a very good player. Whether it's a Duo, Squads, 50 vs. 50, or other team-based game mode, having one or more people invested in winning on your side is a great feeling.

REMEMBER

Fortnite is one of the few games that allows for cross-platform play between many different types of computers, consoles, and mobile devices. Added to the fact that the game is free, this is an easy way to bring your friends and family along, no matter where they might be located.

Communicating effectively

Communication with your teammates is key, so make sure if you're into team-based play that you have a good headset with a microphone or other similar device. See Chapter 2 for some head-set suggestions.

TIP

Don't worry about getting confused in the heat of battle. You can't hurt a teammate and vice-versa. So fire away!

Although you don't want to be too chatty, coordinating attack and defensive strategies, pointing out item locations, or making other key points are all necessary to giving your team the best chance at a victory. So speak up! Just be sure to save the small talk for after the match.

If you're lucky enough to have a regular group of players to team up with, one area where good communication will give you an even bigger advantage is in the construction of large defensive shelters or fortresses. If you can coordinate your actions to collect the necessary materials and then construct the shelter or fortress, you can build structures far more elaborate and defensively sound than any one person would ever have time to build on their own.

Healing injuries and sharing supplies

Besides coordinating strategies, you and your teammates should be there for each other in times of need. For instance, if you or your teammate is badly injured, as long as the health meter doesn't reach zero, there's a chance to be revived. Just make sure you or your teammate act quickly before either an enemy or the dwindling health meter finishes the job first!

Similarly, weapons, ammunition, and other inventory items can be shared as needed, so be sure to spread the wealth. With everyone on your team healthy and wealthy, your chances for a team win go way up, so don't be selfish!

Chapter **4**

Getting to Know the Map

The island is where everything in Battle Royale takes place. Although you would think that being stuck on a single island for eight seasons and counting would get a bit dull, that's hardly the case. It's not only a large island, but it goes through changes — sometimes dramatic changes — each season. This chapter describes how the map is set up and shows you some of the island's highlights. Although this is done through the lens of Season 8's map, these basic techniques to dissect the island can be applied to future seasons as well.

Understanding Map Coordinates

Fortnite's map coordinate system is a bit like algebraic notation (AN) on a chess board. AN identifies each square on a chessboard by a unique coordinate pair, which includes one letter from the top/bottom of the board and one number from the left/right of the board. Unlike a chessboard, which consists of 8 rows by 8 columns totaling 64 squares, the map in Fortnite is divided into 10 by 10 rows totaling 100 squares. Although every square on a chessboard can be played on, some squares on a Fortnite map have little-to-no usable land.

The only other major difference between chess notation and Fortnite notation is that chess notation has numbers 1 through 8 going from bottom to top on the left/right and Fortnite has numbers 1 through 10 going top to bottom. So, this means that the Fortnite equivalent of A8, which is a chessboard's left top-most corner, would instead be A1, as shown in Figure 4-1.

FIGURE 4-1: Fortnite's coordinate system, where A1 is the left top-most corner.

As you can see in Figure 4-1, the Battle Bus is going to stop at I9, which is just after Paradise Palms, found at I8. Note that locations A1, E1, F1, G1, H1, I1, J1, A2, J2, A9, J9, A10, B10, C10, D10, E10, H10, I10, and J10 are mostly water.

Selecting a Starting Location

Your choice of starting location comes down to how you want to approach a particular match. Landing in a crowded area like a city gets you the most loot, which increases your chances for finding the best loot, but it also likely results in the quickest time to battle.

Landing in a remote, less-crowded area like a forest allows you to acquire loot at a more leisurely pace, but you'll have fewer chances at finding the best loot. In addition, there's a good chance you'll be closer to the storm circle, which means you'll have to cover more terrain overall to avoid taking non-combat damage.

If you're a gambler, then landing in a crowded area is your best bet, because it has the biggest payoff but highest risk. If you're more conservative, landing in a remote area has a lower payoff but also lower risk. The major points of interest, their description, and relative risks are discussed in the next section.

Getting to Know the Points of Interest

As of Season 8, there are 20 points of interest named on the map. There are also over a dozen unnamed locations to discover on your own, like the stadium, race track, RV park, and volcano. Whichever season you're in now will have its own locations, although, as with previous seasons, many locations will carry over, and some mostly unchanged.

Northwest points of interest

There are seven major locations in the northwest portion of the Season 8 map, which is shown in Figure 4-2.

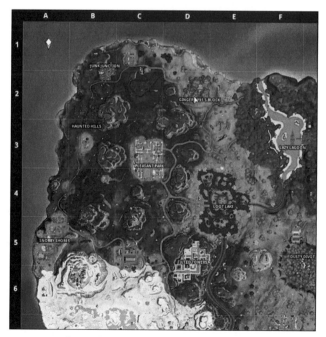

FIGURE 4-2: The northwest points of interest.

The seven major locations are as follows:

>> **Junk Junction:** Location B2. A wrecking yard with plenty of scrap metal and ammo but not a lot of loot. This area is usually not very populated.

>> **The Block:** Location D2. This is where user creations from Creative mode are featured. Note that in Figure 4-2, the *The* in *The Block* is replaced with *Gingerjay91* as *Gingerjay91's Block*.

>> **Haunted Hills:** Location B3. A cemetery with crypts and mausoleums. This is a popular location with high-value loot, particularly inside its buildings.

>> **Pleasant Park:** Location C4. A suburban neighborhood with a football field. This is an extremely popular location with lots of loot and chests.

>> **Loot Lake:** Location E4. A lake with small islands and large, open areas. As the name implies, there are lots of chests and good loot here, but also lots of traffic.

>> **Snobby Shores:** Location A5. A luxury neighborhood with lots of houses to explore.

>> **Tilted Towers:** Location D6. A city with many tall buildings and lots of loot. This is typically the most popular location to land in during a match, so only experienced players should start here.

Northeast points of interest

There are five major locations in the northeast portion of the Season 8 map, which is shown in Figure 4-3.

The five major locations are as follows:

>> **Lazy Lagoon:** Location F3. A pirate ship and a small port with lots of buildings. With lots of loot and weapons, this is a popular destination. Just be careful you don't land in the water!

>> **Sunny Steps:** Location I3. An Aztec-style city with large pyramids and lots of buildings to explore. There are many chests to find and lots of loot to acquire.

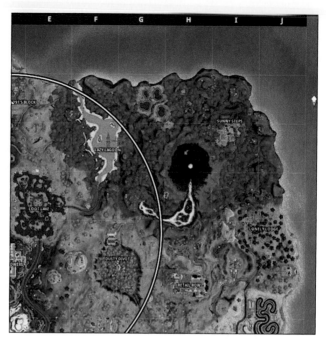

FIGURE 4-3: The northeast points of interest.

>> **Dusty Divot:** Location F5. The location of a meteor impact, it features a diner and other facilities. This tends to be a low-traffic area.

>> **Retail Row:** Location H6. Lots of stores with a sprawling parking lot and a small neighborhood to explore. This is a good place for beginning players to target.

>> **Lonely Lodge:** Location I5. A forested area with a lodge and a watchtower. There's decent loot to be found and only light player traffic.

Southwest points of interest

There are four major locations in the southwest portion of the Season 8 map, which is shown in Figure 4-3.

FIGURE 4-4: The southwest points of interest.

The four major locations are as follows:

>> **Frosty Flights:** Location A8. A large military base. The fighting conditions can be challenging here because of the various buildings to navigate and the location's popularity.

>> **Polar Peak:** Location C8. An iceberg with a large castle fortress complex on top. Ziplines can be used to go up and down the iceberg.

>> **Shifty Shafts:** Location D7. An underground mineshaft complex. Known for lots of loot and close-range combat.

>> **Happy Hamlet:** Location D9. A small town. There are lots of places to get shot from, so only check this area out when you're experienced.

Southeast points of interest

There are four major locations in the southeast portion of the Season 8 map, which is shown in Figure 4-4.

FIGURE 4-5: The southeast points of interest.

The four major locations are as follows:

- ** Salty Springs:** Location F7. A residential area. There's a decent amount of loot and low traffic.

- ** Fatal Fields:** Location F8. A farm complex. The plains can leave you open to long-range fire.

- ** Paradise Palms:** Location I8. A small desert city with a hotel and stores. Check out the hotel for some good loot, but otherwise it's a fairly large, barren area.

- ** Lucky Landing:** Location F10. An Asian-themed town. Although it's a lovely location, it's one of the first places to evacuate after the storm advances.

Chapter **5**

Mastering Weapons, Items, Health, and Defenses

L ike the old saying goes, the best defense is a good offense. This strategic offensive principle of war should be your mantra when competing in the various Battle Royale modes. Although you'll want to protect yourself as much as possible, sooner or later, you'll need to take the fight to your opponents.

This chapter introduces you to weapons and their features, along with some of the other interesting, related items found within the game like traps and explosives. You'll also learn about managing your health and various related defenses.

Understanding Weapon Power and Rarity

Weapons of all types can be found in chests and vending machines, obtained from supply drops, or simply found out in the open as loot, including those dropped by fallen opponents.

Supply drops usually provide the best weapons. These balloons start falling approximately three minutes into the Battle Royale match.

Fortnite rotates weapon selections every season. The game puts a premium on minimizing weapon and functionality duplication, so certain weapons, like other in-game items, get vaulted for a future re-release. Nevertheless, there are certain characteristics that are consistent regardless of how or when specific weapons are introduced: ammunition and rarity.

There are five types of consumable ammunition, from weakest to strongest: light bullets, medium bullets, heavy bullets, shells, and rockets. Each gun requires one specific type of ammunition. For instance, light bullets for handguns, medium bullets for assault rifles, heavy bullets for sniper rifles, shells for shotguns, and rockets for rocket launchers. Ammunition meant for one type of weapon will not work in a different type of weapon. You can carry unlimited ammunition.

There's actually a sixth type of ammunition: arrows! Unfortunately, the crossbows that used it have been vaulted, although you can still use the weapon and ammunition in Creative mode.

Weapon rarity can be distinguished by color, stars, and name. Although name tends to be the most commonly referenced designation among players, a weapon's color appears both when it's on the ground (as its highlight color) and when it's in your inventory (as its background), like in Figure 5-1.

FIGURE 5-1: The second inventory item has an orange background, indicating it's a legendary weapon.

Table 5-1 breaks down weapon color and name designations, from gray and common, like a pistol, all the way to orange and legendary, like a hand cannon. There's also a little used sixth option, gold and mythic, which was first applied to brief appearances by the Infinity Blade and Infinity Gauntlet, the latter a tie-in with the 2018 Marvel film, *Avengers: Infinity War*, where the lucky wielder got to transform into the movie's villain, Thanos.

TIP

The *Avengers: Infinity War* tie-in was just a taste of what Epic Games would eventually unleash for Fortnite's eighth season. For the 2019 film, *Avengers: Endgame*, Epic Games and Marvel unleashed a major crossover event, adding a special Limited Time mode, new skins, and other themed extras, which played a prominent role in the game during the blockbuster film's initial theatrical run. Marvel returned the favor by featuring Fortnite in the film! Expect more blockbuster crossovers in the future.

TABLE 5-1   Weapon Color, Stars, and Name Designations

Color	Name	Stars	Description
Gray	Common	1	Weakest and most common
Green	Uncommon	2	Weak and easier to find
Blue	Rare	3	Strong and hard to find
Purple	Epic	4	Very strong and very hard to find
Orange	Legendary	5	Strongest and most difficult to find
Gold	Mythic	Special icon	Only rarely introduced; has special powers

Generally speaking, the better the rarity, the better a weapon's stats, although having a variety of even weaker weapon types still allows for more flexibility should battle conditions and situations dictate. The next section takes a look at some of these weapon types.

Understanding Weapon Characteristics

As with most of the rest of the game, Fortnite's developers have put a lot of thought into its weapons. For a game with so many fantastic elements, most of the weapons react a lot like their real-world counterparts, backed by individual statistics. You can see an example in Figure 5-2, which shows the stats of a legendary grenade launcher.

TIP

You can check out the stats for the latest weapons and consumables by entering Creative mode and opening the inventory. This mode even showcases some items that are vaulted in Battle Royale!

Legendary | Ranged Weapon

GRENADE LAUNCHER

Ranged | Explosive Weapon

★★★★★

DPS **110.0**

Damage	110.0
Fire Rate	1.0
Magazine Size	6
Reload Time	2.7

FIGURE 5-2: The in-game statistics for a legendary grenade launcher.

Weapons are rated by the following major characteristics:

>> **Rarity:** From common to legendary, and sometimes Mythic, in order of increasing power. Indicated by color, name, and stars. Refer to Table 5-1 for details.

>> **Bullet type:** The type of consumable ammunition a loadable weapon takes, indicated by an icon. The choices are: light bullets, medium bullets, heavy bullets, shells, and rockets.

>> DPS (damage per shot): Some rare weapons can have a lower DPS than more common weapons due to a slower fire rate.

TECHNICAL
STUFF

The actual in-game calculation for DPS is damage times fire rate. For example, a damage value of 27.0 times a fire rate of 3.5 gives you a DPS of 94.5.

>> **Damage:** The actual damage to a character's health from a shot to the body. Depending upon the weapon, a headshot can do the same, double, or more than double the damage that is indicated. When firing on structures, most weapons do at least the same as the indicated damage, and often much more.

TIP

For a better chance at a headshot, or a more accurate shot in general, use a scope if the weapon is equipped with one. If your weapon's scope does not bring an enemy close enough, try switching to a long range weapon, which has a more powerful scope.

TIP

>> **Fire rate:** Number of shots per second.

Although you may think that holding down the fire button to shoot the maximum number of shots per second your weapon allows is a good tactic, that's not always the case. Just like in real life, the longer you hold down the fire button, the wider the bloom, or spray, making your gun harder to control and reducing your accuracy.

>> **Magazine size:** The amount of ammunition held per clip or magazine. The faster you fire a weapon, the quicker you'll go through the ammunition in the clip or magazine.

>> **Reload time:** How long it takes, in seconds, for you to put a new ammunition clip or magazine in your weapon.

TIP

If you're using a gun with a slow reload time and can't hide or take cover, you can switch to a different weapon and fire right away. This quicker action might make all the difference in a tough fire fight!

Short range weapons

Short range weapons, like submachine guns and shotguns, as in Figure 5-3, are ideal for close-quarters combat, like inside and between buildings and other obstacles. These weapons are ineffective at mid range or greater, which is the real-world equivalent of roughly 10 feet or so.

FIGURE 5-3: A pump shotgun.

Table 5-2 provides some example short range weapons and their statistics.

TABLE 5-2 ## Example Short Range Weapons and Statistics

Weapon	Rarity	Bullet Type	DPS	Damage	Fire Rate	Magazine Size	Reload Time
Pistol	Gray – Common – 1 Star	Light Bullets	155.2	23	6.75	16	1.5
Revolver	Green – Uncommon – 2 Stars	Medium Bullets	51.3	57.0	0.9	6	2.3
Pump Shotgun	Blue – Rare – 3 Stars	Shells	70.0	100.0	0.7	5	4.6
Suppressed Pistol	Purple – Epic – 4 Stars	Light Bullets	189.0	28.0	6.75	16	1.3
Double Barrel Shotgun	Orange – Legendary – 5 Stars	Shells	228.0	120.0	1.9	2	2.7

TIP

Weapons that are labeled as *suppressed* muzzle their sounds when fired, making it more difficult for other players to locate you.

TIP

Shotguns are a favorite close combat weapon because they pack a great deal of power and have a decent fire rate. The major downsides, however, are that they don't hold much ammo and take some time to reload.

Mid range weapons

Mid range weapons, like light machine guns and assault rifles, as in Figure 5-4, are ideal for most standard combat situations, where versatility and a high rate of fire can make all the difference between life and death. Using these weapons at short range or long range reduces their accuracy. Table 5-3 provides some example mid range weapons and their statistics.

FIGURE 5-4: An assault rifle.

TABLE 5-3 **Example Mid Range Weapons and Statistics**

Weapon	Rarity	Bullet Type	DPS	Damage	Fire Rate	Magazine Size	Reload Time
Heavy Assault Rifle	Gray – Common – 1 Star	Medium Bullets	135.0	36.0	3.75	25	3.1
Hunting Rifle	Green – Uncommon – 2 Stars	Heavy Bullets	68.8	86.0	0.8	1	1.9
Infantry Rifle	Blue – Rare – 3 Stars	Medium Bullets	168.0	42.0	4.0	8	2.3
Suppressed Assault Rifle	Purple – Epic – 4 Stars	Medium Bullets	176.0	32.0	5.5	30	2.2
Minigun	Orange – Legendary – 5 Stars	Light Bullets	228.0	19.0	12	Unlimited	4.5

TIP

Some weapons, like the minigun, overheat after a set number of consecutive rounds are fired, so something that appears to be a serious advantage, like unlimited ammo, still has its limits. Remember, there are pluses and minuses to every weapon!

Long range weapons

Long range weapons, like sniper rifles, as in Figure 5-5, are ideal for wide open spaces where you can get a clean shot at your opponent from far away. Although long range weapons can be used at close range, they're most effective at mid range or greater, particularly since they're slow to reload. Table 5-4 provides some example long range weapons and their statistics.

FIGURE 5-5: A heavy sniper rifle.

TIP

Because of their relative power, there are no common long range weapons, so you'll need to be extra diligent to find one!

TABLE 5-4 Example Long Range Weapons and Statistics

Weapon	Rarity	Bullet Type	DPS	Damage	Fire Rate	Magazine Size	Reload Time
Semi-Auto Sniper Rifle	Green – Uncommon – 2 Stars	Heavy Bullets	90.0	75.0	1.2	10	2.5
Bolt-Action Sniper Rifle	Blue – Rare – 3 Stars	Heavy Bullets	34.7	105.0	0.33	1	3.0
Suppressed Sniper Rifle	Purple – Epic – 4 Stars	Heavy Bullets	33.0	100.0	0.33	1	2.8
Heavy Sniper Rifle	Orange – Legendary – 5 Stars	Heavy Bullets	51.8	157.0	0.33	1	4.1

Other weapons

Although you'll primarily find and want to stick with guns, there are several other weapon types to choose from. (See Figure 5-6.) Examples include crossbows, rocket and grenade launchers, and grenades, the latter of which we'll cover later in this chapter in the section "Learning to Aim Projectiles and Explosives." Table 5-5 provides some examples of these weapon types and their statistics.

FIGURE 5-6: A rocket launcher.

TIP

Many of these other weapons feature explosive damage and can damage everything in their blast radius, including you. Use caution!

TABLE 5-5 ## Example Other Weapons and Statistics

Weapon	Rarity	Bullet Type	DPS	Damage	Fire Rate	Magazine Size	Reload Time
Grenade Launcher	Blue – Rare – 3 Stars	Rockets	100.0	100.0	1.0	6	3.0
Rocket Launcher	Purple – Epic – 4 Stars	Rockets	87.0	116.0	0.75	1	3.4
Boom Bow	Orange – Legendary – 5 Stars	Shells	115.0	115.0	1.0	1	1.3

Learning to Aim Guns

If your plan is to shoot indiscriminately at anything that moves, you're likely to have little success. There are select principles that you can follow to increase your hit, and kill, rates:

>> **Go for the head.** No matter what weapon you're using, getting a headshot will almost always cause more damage than a shot to the body. Of course, hitting the body is much easier, so you'll need to weigh your chances of success at a headshot before pulling the trigger.

>> **Get in close.** Unless you're using a Long Range weapon like a sniper rifle or some type of explosive, the closer you are to your target when you open fire, the better. You can not only increase your accuracy, but can also cause more damage.

>> **Stand your ground.** Although you sometimes can't avoid remaining in motion, if you can stand still before firing, the accuracy of your aim increases. If you crouch and remain still, your accuracy increases even further.

>> **Aim.** Press the Aim Down Sights button to aim at your target before firing.

Of course, arguably the most important principle for success in that list is to aim, but it's important to know how it's influenced by the other factors. Bullets hit anywhere within the aiming reticule, so the smaller the reticule, the more accurate your bullets.

Figure 5-7 shows the size of the aiming reticule when running. It's at its largest size.

Figure 5-8 shows the size of the aiming reticule when standing still. Note that it's much smaller than when running.

Figure 5-9 shows the size of the aiming reticule when crouching and moving. It's smaller than when standing still.

Figure 5-10 shows the size of the aiming reticule when crouching and staying still. It's at its smallest size.

FIGURE 5-7: The aiming reticule is large when running.

FIGURE 5-8: The aiming reticule is average size when standing still.

FIGURE 5-9: The aiming reticule is on the smaller side when crouching and moving.

FIGURE 5-10: The aiming reticule is at its smallest size when crouching and staying still.

Although it's been stated before, it's rarely a good idea to hold down the fire button and continuously fire your weapon. Figure 5-11 shows how big the reticule is when standing and firing a single shot.

FIGURE 5-11: Firing a single shot keeps the targeting reticule at a smaller size.

Figure 5-12 shows how that same reticule increases in size as the bloom, or bullet spray, increases. It becomes increasingly inaccurate, so shoot in shorter bursts.

FIGURE 5-12: Firing multiple shots increases the size of the targeting reticule and disperses your shots over a wider range, further decreasing accuracy.

Regardless of posture or motion, if you really want the most accurate shot, press the Aim button. Figure 5-13 shows how small the aiming reticule is when standing and pressing the Aim button.

FIGURE 5-13: Standing and pressing the Aim button results in the smallest possible aiming reticule.

Figure 5-14 shows what happens when moving and aiming. The aiming reticule is still quite small, but becomes darker, indicating slightly less accuracy.

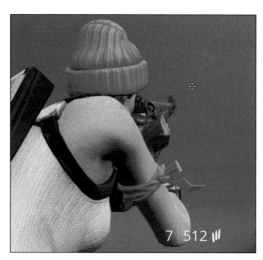

FIGURE 5-14: Moving and pressing the Aim button results in a still small aiming reticule, but one that's more susceptible to bloom than staying still.

Finally, when sniping, as seen in Figure 5-15, you'll need to be wary of a phenomenon called *bullet drop*. Just like in the real world, when a bullet travels long distances, around 100 yards and more, it drops a bit as the force of gravity acts upon it. Although there's no way to avoid bullet drop entirely, generally speaking, the heavier the weapon, like the heavy sniper rifle, the less susceptible it is to this phenomena and the less you'll have to cheat your aim up.

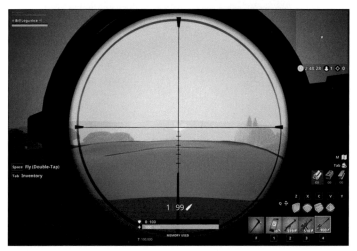

FIGURE 5-15: If you get a sniper rifle and aim, the very distant suddenly becomes very close.

Learning to Aim Projectiles and Explosives

Rocket and grenade launchers are powerful weapons. They can not only take down structures, but also anyone unlucky enough to be in or near them.

Standard rocket launchers, like the one shown in Figure 5-16, work just like a regular gun. Aim and fire.

TIP

Because you need some distance for a projectile to be effective, try not to shoot straight-on to where an enemy is looking. They'll likely be able to see the missile coming and take evasive action like building a wall or dropping a launch pad. Try to surprise your target from behind.

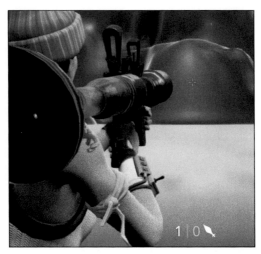

FIGURE 5-16: Aiming a rocket launcher.

If you're lucky enough to come across a guide missile launcher, you also aim it like normal. However, after you pull the trigger, you can steer the missile in the air using your regular movement controls.

When using a grenade launcher, like shown in Figure 5-17, the targeting system has two lines below the aiming circle. Those two lines indicate the projectile will fall in a downward arc. Other projectile weapons, like the quad launcher, use the same targeting system.

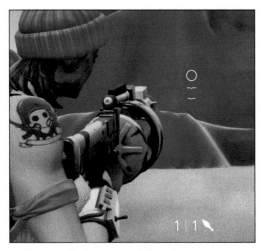

FIGURE 5-17: Aiming a grenade launcher.

Handheld projectiles, like grenades, also use the same targeting system, but the arc it will travel appears as a blue line, as shown in Figure 5-18. The obvious difference between a weapon-launched projectile and one you throw is that thrown objects travel a shorter distance.

FIGURE 5-18: Aiming a grenade.

The final factor to keep in mind when firing or throwing a grenade is bounce. As you can see in Figure 5-19, a grenade will bounce one or more times after it hits a solid object.

FIGURE 5-19: A grenade bounces off of solid objects.

You'll need to get a sense of the timing for a grenade's explosion, like in Figure 5-20, to use it most effectively.

FIGURE 5-20: You'll need to learn the timing of when a grenade will explode after bouncing off solid objects.

Here are some of the special grenade types you may find in the game and their characteristics:

>> **Boogie bomb:** Does no damage upon exploding, but forces an opponent (or you, like in Figure 5-21!) to dance helplessly for five seconds. You can stack up to ten boogie bombs in one inventory slot.

>> **Clinger grenade:** Works like a regular grenade, but sticks to and stays on whatever it first hits instead of bouncing. You can stack up to six clinger grenades in one inventory slot.

>> **Dynamite:** Thrown like a grenade with a five-second timer, up to ten dynamite bundles can be retained in one inventory slot.

>> **Impulse grenade:** Does no damage upon exploding, but launches a player in the opposite direction of the impact. You can stack up to nine impulse grenades in one inventory slot.

FIGURE 5-21: A boogie bomb leaves a player — and you, if caught in the blast — helpless for five seconds.

>> **Remote explosives:** Thrown like a grenade, you detonate the explosive with your remote when ready. You can stack up to six remote explosives in one inventory slot.

>> **Shockwave grenade:** A more powerful version of the impulse grenade. You can stack up to six shockwave grenades in one inventory slot.

>> **Stink bomb:** Thrown like a grenade, upon exploding it generates a temporary toxic cloud of yellow smoke, as shown in Figure 5-22, which causes damage for every half-second a player is caught within it. You can stack up to six stink bombs in one inventory slot.

FIGURE 5-22: A stink bomb cloud.

Managing Your Health and Maximizing Defenses

Consumables that raise or augment your health and shield are some of the more underrated items for newer Fortnite players. Although it's easy to focus on the best weapons and offensive strategies for using them, you will still get shot at. A lot. It's how you manage being attacked that will allow you to eventually land the winning blows against your opponents.

Understanding healing and shield items

Your Health stat is the green bar or meter after the plus icon. It indicates the number of hit points (HP) you have, out of 100. Each time you get hit, both the green bar and the actual number go down to indicate damage. If your damage reaches zero, you're dead.

Your Shield stat is the bar after the shield icon and just above the Health bar, as shown in Figure 5-23. It indicates the number of shield points (SP) out of 100. When your shield is down to zero points, you have no additional protection and will take direct health damage. You start out each Battle Royale match with no shield points.

Shield bar

Health bar

FIGURE 5-23: The green Health and Shield bars are stacked one on top of the other. The Shield stat shown indicates there are 25 out of a possible 100 shield points.

You can pick up several items to improve either your health or shield stats, and sometimes both. Because each item takes up an inventory slot, it's best to use their effects as soon as possible. Foraged healing items, like apples and coconuts, can't be stored in inventory, so must be consumed immediately.

What follows are some of important health and shield items you may come across and their usage:

>> **Bandage:** Up to 15 can be carried in one inventory slot. Each bandage takes 4 seconds to apply and raises your health by 15 HP, up to a maximum of 75 HP. (See Figure 5-24.)

FIGURE 5-24: Bandage.

>> **Cozy campfire:** This one is especially suited for team play. Although technically classified as a trap that can only be set on a floor you've built, it will generate up to 50 HP at a rate of 2 HP per second for you and your squad mates over a duration of 25 seconds.

You can take being a good squad mate to the next level with the Reboot Van. Your fallen comrades will drop reboot cards that any surviving member can then take to a Reboot Van and spawn their teammates back into the game.

>> **Med Kit:** Up to three can be carried in one inventory slot. Each med kit takes 10 seconds to apply, but will always bring you back to a full 100 HP. (See Figure 5-25.)

FIGURE 5-25: Med kit.

>> **Apple:** This foraged item is usually found under trees and must be consumed immediately. Each apple takes 1 second to consume and heals for 5 HP.

>> **Banana:** This foraged item is found in tropical biomes and must be consumed immediately. (See Figure 5-26.) Each banana takes 1 second to consume and heals for 5 HP.

FIGURE 5-26: Banana.

>> **Coconut:** This foraged item is usually found in palm trees and must be consumed immediately. Each coconut takes 1 second to consume and heals for 5 HP. If your HP is already full, your SP will restore for 5 SP.

>> **Mushroom:** This foraged item is found on the ground and must be consumed immediately. Each mushroom takes 1 second to consume and heals for 5 HP.

>> **Pepper:** This foraged item is usually found on the ground and must be consumed immediately. Each pepper takes 1 second to consume and heals for 5 HP. There's also a secondary effect of a 20 percent increase in movement speed that lasts for 10 seconds.

>> **Small shield potion:** Up to 10 can be carried in one inventory slot. Each small shield potion takes 2 seconds to consume and raises your SP by 25 points, up to a maximum of 50. (See Figure 5-27.)

FIGURE 5-27: Small shield potion.

>> **Shield potion:** Up to three can be carried in one inventory slot. Each shield potion takes 5 seconds to consume and raises your SP by 50 points, up to the maximum of 100. (See Figure 5-28.)

FIGURE 5-28: Shield potion.

>> **Slurp juice:** Up to two can be carried in one inventory slot. Each slurp juice takes 2 seconds to consume and restores up to 75 HP and 75 SP at a rate of 2 per second over its 37.5-second effect duration. (See Figure 5-29.)

FIGURE 5-29: Slurp juice.

>> **Chug jug:** Only one of this legendary consumable can be carried in one inventory slot. Each chug jug takes 15 seconds to consume and restores up to 100 HP and 100 SP. (See Figure 5-30.)

FIGURE 5-30: Chug jug.

Understanding camouflage and defensive items

Defense in Fortnite has a lot to do with staying mobile, keeping your options open, and building defensive structures on the fly. However, as you should expect from Fortnite, there are still many other interesting ways to become a defensive master.

TIP

All Fortnite characters are right-handed. This means you overlook your character's right shoulder, which affects how you cover your body. If you peek out of cover from the left side rather than right, you'll have to expose your entire body to fight. Keep this right-handed bias in mind so you expose as little of your body as possible!

Let's take a look at some of these clever defensive options:

>> **Bouncer:** A pad trap, the Bouncer, as shown in Figure 5-31, can be placed on any ramp or flat surface and launches you or an opponent into the air. When the player lands, they'll suffer no damage. When acquired, this trap is accessible from Build mode.

>> **Bush:** Up to two bushes can be in one inventory slot. After consuming this item and waiting three seconds, you will turn into a bush, like shown in Figure 5-32. To your opponents, you'll be a regular bush, so be careful when you move. If shot at, you lose the disguise.

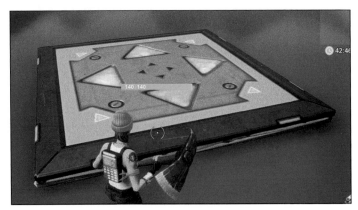

FIGURE 5-31: A bouncer trap.

FIGURE 5-32: Disguised as a bush.

>> **Damage trap:** These traps, shown in Figure 5-33, can be placed on any floor, wall, or ceiling and activates when a player walks by, dealing 150 HP of damage. It takes five seconds for the trap to reset and can only be removed when the surface it's placed on is destroyed. When acquired, this trap is accessible from Build mode.

FIGURE 5-33: A damage Trap.

>> **Grappler:** Classified as an epic ranged weapon, the grappler takes one inventory slot and has ten shots. Use it to grab onto a nearby object and catapult yourself forward. It's great for quick escapes or to reach higher or lower elevations. If you're out of range of a suitable target, there will be a red X in place of the target cross-hairs, which are shown in Figure 5-34.

FIGURE 5-34: Activating a grappler after its target is in range.

>> **Launch pad:** Similar to the bouncer, but giving even more of a boost, the launch pad is a favorite way to travel long distances as quickly as possible. When acquired, this trap is accessible from Build mode.

Fortnite uses not only visual cues but also sound cues, for almost every in-game action. Make a point to learn what different sounds mean, so you know where enemy activity is coming from. Of course, other players can make use of these same cues, so be careful using any type of weapon, device, or other item that really makes its presence known.

» **Mounted turret:** Placeable on any floor tile, the mounted turret, shown in Figure 5-35, has unlimited ammunition, but can overheat. Any player can use the mounted turret once placed, so implement such a powerful defensive weapon with such awesome offensive capabilities with caution. When acquired, this trap is accessible from Build mode.

FIGURE 5-35: Inside a mounted turret.

» **Port-a-fort:** Classified as a grenade, the port-a-fort spawns a pre-made fort upon impact. It's three stories tall and made of metal, so it saves a lot of build time and is also hard to destroy. Tires on the bottom floor allow you to quickly jump up to the roof. You can store up to five Port-a-Forts in one inventory slot.

» **Port-a-fortress:** A supersized port-a-fort, the port-a-fortress, shown in Figure 5-36, features bouncers to make quick escapes.

FIGURE 5-36: The inside of a port-a-fortress.

>> **Rift-to-go:** The ultimate getaway tool, the rift-to-go creates a rift that teleports you back into the sky. (See Figure 5-37.) Up to two of these snow globes can be placed in one inventory slot.

FIGURE 5-37: A rift-to-go.

IN THIS CHAPTER

» Understanding raw materials

» Harvesting raw materials

» Building simple structures

» Editing structures

» Building with purpose

» Working with Creative mode

Chapter **6**

Building and Creating in Fortnite

t's undeniably important to know how to use the various weapons and defensive items described in Chapter 5, but building is the real differentiator between those who simply compete and those who compete to win. If you can master this creative and fun process, your chances at a Victory Royale go up significantly.

In this chapter you learn about the various materials and how and why to build and edit structures. Finally, you learn a bit more about Creative mode, where you can safely flex your burgeoning creative muscles.

Understanding Raw Materials

The foundation of any structure is its raw materials. In Fortnite, three unique raw materials are used for building: wood, stone, and metal. Almost every in-game object, including buildings, trees, vehicles, rocks, and crates, can be broken down and harvested for one or more of these raw materials.

If you have enough of a particular raw material, you can build new structures of your own, from walls and ramps to entire buildings. Each material has its own set of properties and its own *spawn time*, which is how long it takes for the material to finish setting and reach its full strength.

Let's take a look at these raw materials and some of their key properties:

>> **Wood:** The weakest of the three raw materials, but the quickest to harvest and build with and the most abundant. Wood, shown in Figure 6-1, also has the highest starting health at 100 HP, but lowest maximum health. You can harvest wood from trees, furniture, pallets, walls, and more. At full build, which requires a spawn time of up to seven seconds, wood has 200 HP.

FIGURE 6-1: Wood.

>> **Stone:** Stone, shown in Figure 6-2, falls squarely in the middle of raw material properties. It's slower to harvest than wood, but stronger, and it's faster to harvest than metal, but weaker. You can harvest stone from rocks, walls, roofs, chimneys, and more. At full build, which requires a spawn time of up to fifteen seconds, Stone has 300 HP, versus a starting health of 90 HP.

TIP

You'll sometimes see stone referred to by others as brick because the icon looks like a brick and the stones are assembled like brick. It's still always labeled as stone in-game.

FIGURE 6-2: Stone.

>> **Metal:** Metal, shown in Figure 6-3, is the strongest material at full build, but it starts out weak, with just 80 HP, because of an extended spawn time. You can harvest metal from vehicles, fences, shipping containers, crates, and more. At full build, which requires up to 30 seconds, metal has 400 HP.

TIP

Like stone with brick, you'll sometimes see metal referred to as steel. It's still always labeled as metal in-game.

FIGURE 6-3: Metal.

Health points vary by the type of structure you ultimately build, but the stronger the material used, the more HP the structure will have. Although using stronger materials means a longer build time for you, it also means your enemies will have to use more firepower to take down your structures. As with most things in Fortnite, material usage can be a real balancing act that requires experience only in-game trial and error can provide.

Harvesting Raw Materials

Although you'll sometimes want to use your weapons to bring down structures other players are occupying or using for protection, it's your pickaxe that's always the best tool for the harvesting of raw materials. Over the course of a game you can also collect raw materials from chests and fallen enemies.

To harvest a raw material with your pickaxe, follow these steps:

1. **Ready your pickaxe and get close to and face your object, like in Figure 6-4.**

    The targeting crosshairs should be centered on your object.

FIGURE 6-4: Facing a tree to harvest the wood raw material.

2. **Repeatedly strike your target object with the pickaxe, like in Figure 6-5.**

    As you collect the raw material, a notification indicating how much you're actively harvesting appears to your character's left and your respective material inventory count increases.

FIGURE 6-5: Striking an object with the pickaxe.

3. **Position your crosshair over the blue targeting circle, like in Figure 6-6, and continue striking your target object.**

FIGURE 6-6: Aligning the crosshair with the blue targeting circle makes harvesting much more efficient.

Aiming for and hitting the blue targeting circle, which appears after your first strike, makes harvesting faster and your strikes more powerful, as shown in Figure 6-7. Each time you hit the blue targeting circle, you hear a ding, and it moves to another location. Keep after the blue targeting circle until your target object is completely harvested or you have enough of the desired raw material.

FIGURE 6-7: A perfect strike results in more material harvested.

Using the pickaxe without hitting the blue targeting circle does 50 points of damage to an object. Using the pickaxe and hitting the blue targeting circle does 100 points of damage to an object.

Larger objects have more HP than smaller objects, but they also provide more raw materials. For instance, a small tree with 200 HP might provide 20 wood, whereas a large tree with 800 HP might provide 210 wood.

TIP

As you go around harvesting various objects, make a mental note of their starting total HP. Those same objects provide the same amount of protection from enemy fire should you need to take cover behind one of them.

When you have acquired your desired number of each raw material, as shown in the example in Figure 6-8, you can start building structures. This process is explained in the next section.

FIGURE 6-8: A healthy number of raw materials in inventory in a late stage of a Battle Royale match.

Building Simple Structures

There are four building types in Fortnite: walls, floors, ramps, and pyramids. Each of these four simple structures, along with a fifth slot for traps, is shown above your inventory, ready for access, like in Figure 6-9.

TIP

You'll sometimes see ramps referred to by others as stairs because the icon looks like steps and is assembled like stairs when using any raw material except for wood. It's still always labeled as ramp in-game.

FIGURE 6-9: The four simple structure types are above your inventory. The fifth slot is for traps.

TIP

The easiest way to follow along is to select Creative mode and go to your blank island. You'll be able to build without being harassed by other players.

You can manually enter Build mode or select one of the simple structures to automatically switch to Build mode. Figure 6-10 shows what happens when you select a structure, in this case a wall.

FIGURE 6-10: Selecting a wall.

After a structure is selected, you'll see a blue silhouette of the basic shape. Until you select Build, you can manipulate the structure's properties.

Let's take a look at a simple structure's options, shown in Figure 6-11, prior to placement with the Build option:

FIGURE 6-11: A simple structure's options.

>> **HP:** The number of health points a structure has, which is based on both its type and its material. The HP breakdown is as follows:

- *Wall:* wood = 150 HP, stone = 300 HP, metal = 500 HP
- *Floor:* wood = 140 HP, stone = 280 HP, metal = 460 HP
- *Ramp:* wood = 140 HP, stone = 280 HP, metal = 460 HP
- *Pyramid:* wood = 140 HP, stone = 280 HP, metal = 460 HP

>> **Edit:** Allows you to turn squares within the structure on or off, either before or after placing the structure with the Build option. The edit function is described in detail in the next section.

>> **Build:** Shows the currently select raw material and how much of that material is required. Selecting Build places the structure at the current location. If a location is invalid, the placement crosshairs will turn red, like in Figure 6-12.

FIGURE 6-12: If a structure can't be placed in a particular location, the placement crosshair turns red.

>> **Material:** Switch raw building materials between wood, stone, and metal.

>> **Rotate:** Rotate the object in place.

Because building during a Battle Royale match requires speed and efficiency, there are two options you should turn on under the Control Options, described in Chapter 2, to help automate the process. The first is Turbo Building and the second is Automatic Material Change, both shown in Figure 6-13.

Set both of these options to on for faster builds

FIGURE 6-13: Both Turbo Building and Automatic Material Change should be set to On.

Turbo Building lets you hold down the fire button to build structures quickly. Automatic Material Change complements Turbo Building by automatically moving onto and using the next raw material when you run out of the currently selected raw material.

Regardless of how you automate your controls, the basic build process remains the same and is more or less reflective of how structures are assembled in the real world, just much faster. Let's use the building of a small shack as our first example, making sure you first have sufficient raw materials, like wood:

1. **Make sure you have open space to build and then select a wall, as shown in Figure 6-14.**

2. **Click Build to place the wall.**

   The wall is now in place, as shown in Figure 6-15.

FIGURE 6-14: There's enough open space to place both the wall and build the final structure.

FIGURE 6-15: The first wall has been built.

3. **Place and build a second wall to left of the first wall, as shown in Figure 6-16.**

4. **Place and build a third wall to the left of second wall, as shown in Figure 6-17.**

   You may need to move your character closer to first two walls to position this third wall correctly.

FIGURE 6-16: The second wall.

FIGURE 6-17: The third wall.

5. **Place and build the fourth and final wall to the left of the third wall and to the right of the first wall, as shown in Figure 6-18.**

The small shack now has four walls, so it's time to add a roof.

FIGURE 6-18: The fourth wall (not for breaking).

6. **Select a pyramid and aim it above the walls, as shown in Figure 6-19.**

TIP

Despite the name, a floor tile also works as a roof, but it is mostly intended to add another level to a structure.

FIGURE 6-19: Aiming a pyramid to make a roof.

7. **Click Build to place the roof.**

Your structure is now complete, as shown in Figure 6-20.

FIGURE 6-20: A complete structure.

Or is it? Without a door, there's no way out without destroying a wall! Although we'll go into more detail on how to edit structures in the next section, follow these steps for now to add a way out:

1. **Face a wall, as shown in Figure 6-21, and make sure you have a wall selected in Build mode.**

The Edit option appears.

2. **Click Edit.**

The editing grid appears, as in Figure 6-22.

3. **Aim at and press fire on the bottom block.**

The bottom block is greyed out, as in Figure 6-23.

4. **Click Confirm.**

There's now an opening you can crouch-walk through, as shown in Figure 6-24.

FIGURE 6-21: The Edit option appears when facing a structure you can edit.

FIGURE 6-22: The editing grid.

FIGURE 6-23: The bottom block is selected for removal.

FIGURE 6-24: There's now an opening!

You now know the basics of building simple structures. Let's take a look at editing structures in a bit more detail in the next section before we tackle some more advanced builds.

Editing Structures

Editing, like building, is an important skill in Fortnite. Without solid editing skills, you won't be able to make the more elaborate structures needed to compete against the game's best players.

Any of the simple structures, such as walls, floors, ramps, and pyramids, can be edited. Each of these four structures is made of either a 2 x 2 or 3 x 3 grid of squares, each of which can be edited either before or after placement through the Edit command.

Structures that you or your teammates build can be edited. Any structures not built by you or your teammates can't be edited, only damaged or destroyed.

When in editing mode, valid edits are indicated in blue. When you mark a square block for removal, it turns grey. If you try an illegal edit that would result in an unsustainable structure, the remaining blocks will turn red, as in Figure 6-25. Either correct the error or select Reset to bring the simple structure back to its original configuration.

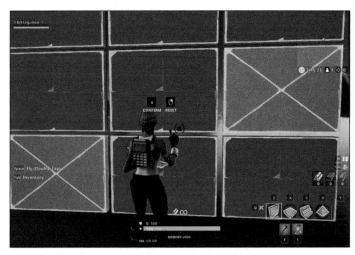

FIGURE 6-25: Although removal of the middle right block was legal, removal of the bottom left block was not, making any edits invalid and turning the rest of the grid red.

Fortnite automatically keeps your last edit, so you can keep holding the button down to repeat your previous build design.

TIP

Editing walls

You can add a window or door to any wall, which consists of a 3 x 3 grid. Follow these steps:

1. **Select the wall in Build mode, like in Figure 6-26.**

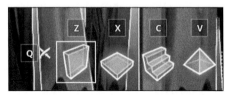

FIGURE 6-26: A wall is selected in Build mode.

2. **Build a wall or stand in front of an existing wall.**

   If you're building a new wall, you can wait to place it.

3. **Click Edit.**

   The editing grid appears, as in Figure 6-27.

FIGURE 6-27: The editing grid.

4. **Aim at and press fire on any single blocks where you'd like a window, or on any two blocks, one on top of the other, where you'd like a door, as shown in Figure 6-28.**

FIGURE 6-28: Selecting two blocks, one on top of the other, to make a door.

5. **Click Confirm.**

Your door or window is now placed, as shown in Figure 6-29.

FIGURE 6-29: A completed door.

You can lower or shorten a wall by following the preceding process and editing out an entire row of three blocks, as shown in Figure 6-30.

FIGURE 6-30: The same wall with the top row of three blocks removed.

What can be taken out can also be put back, as long as it results in a stable structure. Simply edit the structure again and aim at and press fire on any of the empty blocks you'd like replaced.

Although of somewhat questionable value during battle, you can make half a wall by removing the three corner blocks from either side, as in Figure 6-31.

FIGURE 6-31: Removing the three left corner blocks to make a left sloping wall.

This removal results in a triangular wall, as in Figure 6-32.

FIGURE 6-32: A triangular wall.

Editing floors

Editing a floor is a lot like editing a wall but with a smaller 2 x 2 grid. Editing out one to three floor blocks results in a matching hole in the floor, protected by guard rails. The example in Figure 6-33 has the upper-left tile edited out, providing an opening down to the floor below.

If you edit out two diagonally opposing floor blocks — like, say, the top-left and bottom-right blocks — you get the bridge-like structure shown in Figure 6-34.

Editing ramps

Ramps are the most complicated of the simple structures to edit. Although you can't remove any tiles from its 3 x 3 grid, you do have to determine angle, thickness, and direction. To edit a ramp, like in Figure 6-35, select, hold, and drag from one section to another.

FIGURE 6-33: An opening from the second floor down into the first floor.

FIGURE 6-34: Removing two diagonally opposing floor blocks results in this bridge-like structure.

FIGURE 6-35: Editing a ramp, which shows the default arrow configuration.

To create a half-ramp, select, hold, and drag from the bottom corner up to the top corner of the same row, as shown in Figure 6-36.

FIGURE 6-36: Making a half-ramp.

A completed half-ramp is shown in Figure 6-37.

FIGURE 6-37: A finished half-ramp.

To create an L-shaped ramp, select, hold, and drag from the bottom corner up to the top corner of the same row, then continue to the opposite corner, as shown in Figure 6-38.

A completed L-shaped ramp is shown in Figure 6-39.

To create a U-shaped ramp, select, hold, and drag from the bottom corner up to the top corner of the same row and then follow around until you reach the opposite bottom corner, as shown in Figure 6-40.

A completed U-shaped ramp is shown in Figure 6-41.

FIGURE 6-38: Making an L-shaped ramp.

FIGURE 6-39: A finished L-shaped ramp.

FIGURE 6-40: Making a U-shaped ramp.

FIGURE 6-41: A finished U-shaped ramp.

Editing pyramids

A pyramid, like a ramp, is an unusual structure to edit. The pieces in its 2 x 2 grid, shown in Figure 6-42, can't be removed, but they can be raised and then lowered.

If you raise one corner, as in Figure 6-42, you get a ridge.

FIGURE 6-42: Raising one corner square in a pyramid edit.

A ridge pyramid is shown in Figure 6-43.

FIGURE 6-43: A finished ridge pyramid.

If you raise two side-by-side squares, as in Figure 6-44, you get a ramp.

FIGURE 6-44: Raising two side-by-side squares in a pyramid edit.

A ramp pyramid is shown in Figure 6-45.

FIGURE 6-45: A finished ramp pyramid.

If you raise three squares, as in Figure 6-46, you get a concave shape that only stays up if it has at least two walls to attach to.

FIGURE 6-46: Raising three squares in a pyramid edit.

A concave pyramid is shown in Figure 6-47.

FIGURE 6-47: A finished concave pyramid.

Building with Purpose

Building is a great, and fun, general-purpose tool in Fortnite. However, when in a heated Battle Royale match, it's always important to build with a goal in mind. Throw up a quick wall to absorb enemy fire. Build a bridge to span both height and distance. Create a lookout post to both spot and snipe at enemies. And so much more.

Let's take a look at some ways to build with purpose in Fortnite:

>> **Double ramp:** Build two ramps, side-by-side. You can move back and forth between the ramps depending upon the side you're being attacked from, and, if one ramp gets destroyed, you can jump over to the surviving ramp instead of plummeting down into potential damage and danger.

TIP

If components of your structure have taken damage and you're no longer under immediate threat, it may make sense to use the Repair command rather than to start over somewhere else.

>> **Hunter's perch:** Build a tower with a ramp pyramid on top, like the one shown in Figure 6-48. This build gives you the all-important height advantage and provides protection for your sides and rear.

FIGURE 6-48: A hunter's perch build.

>> **Panic fort:** Although it's not as quick as simply throwing up a wall between you and an enemy, a panic fort is still a fast build and is considerably more versatile, providing both protection and some height. To build a panic fort, like the one shown in Figure 6-49, build a wall between you and the enemy, then build the three other walls. Finally, place a ramp right under you in the direction of the enemy.

FIGURE 6-49: A panic fort.

>> **Panic ramp:** To get away fast, build panic ramps. They give you a height advantage and also protect you against enemies facing the underside of the ramp. For extra protection, throw up occasional side walls on the way up.

REMEMBER

Weak foundations are the bane of complex structures. If an enemy takes out the foundation, then your whole structure will come tumbling down. Be especially weary of any type of explosive attacks!

>> **Panic wall:** This is the most common form of defense. When under direct attack, throw up a wall to absorb the damage. Walls can also slow down pursuing enemies, particularly when placed in already densely packed environments.

TIP

You can build just about anywhere, even on top of existing structures and buildings. Never hesitate to take advantage of what's around you!

>> **Scissor ramp:** Sometimes referred to as an over-under ramp, a scissor ramp is where you put a ramp both under and over you in an alternating build, like shown in Figure 6-50. This protects you from attacks from higher elevations until you gain the height you need. This defensive technique is particularly useful when trying to make it up a mountain and you're unsure of enemy positions.

FIGURE 6-50: A scissor ramp.

>> **Simple bridge:** Like a panic wall, simple bridges are an elegant solution to a common problem. If you need to speed across a span of water, mountains, or buildings to make it to the other side, simply lay down floors as you go. Each new section will be held up by the previous section. This works great when holding down the Build button, just make sure you have enough resources to span longer distances!

TIP

Traps are used like any other building material and can be placed not only on floors, but also on ceilings and walls. Get creative with trap placement in and around your builds to surprise your enemies!

As you get more advanced, you can build even more interesting structures. For instance, follow these steps to build a sniper-friendly tower base for you and your teammates:

1. **Build four walls around you as you remain in the middle. If the ground is not level, add a floor.**

   You now have a four-wall structure, as in Figure 6-51.

FIGURE 6-51: A four-wall structure.

2. **Select the ramp.**
3. **Jump and then press Build to stay on top of the ramp, as in Figure 6-52.**
4. **Walk to the top of the ramp and build four more walls.**
5. **Repeat steps 1–4 until you reach your desired height.**
6. **Add a floor.**

7. **When you're at your desired height, add a roof, as shown in Figure 6-53.**

8. **At the top floor, add eight windows, two to a side, as in Figure 6-54.**

   You should now have a great view of your surroundings, ready to torment your enemies from above.

FIGURE 6-52: Stay on the top of the ramp to continue building.

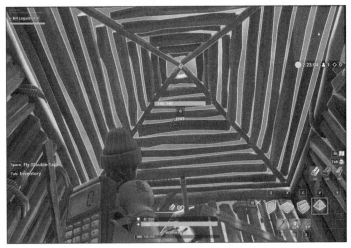

FIGURE 6-53: The top of the structure is finished off with a roof.

FIGURE 6-54: The complete structure as seen from the outside.

TIP

Although not as important as it once was, building a fort or base with other players is a great exercise in communication and teamwork and still an impressive defensive position, particularly if built in the center of the map at the later stages of a match.

Putting It All Together in Creative Mode

Other massively popular video games, like *Minecraft*, have long-since proven the value of having an enemy-free construction mode. Although it took Epic Games until December 2018 to implement such a mode in Fortnite, it didn't disappoint. Creative mode lets you play around in the Battle Royale map as well as with the creations of others, either alone or with friends and family. Perhaps the best part, though, is that you're given your very own blank island to do with as you please. It's the ultimate sandbox environment!

When you first enter Creative mode, you're placed in the Hub. Directly in front of you is an option for your own, blank island, as in Figure 6-55. Up the stairs are the current featured creations you can explore and play with. Directly behind you are sections of the Battle Royale map you can be dropped over, like Pleasant Park, Polar Peak, Dusty Divot, Paradise Palms, and Sunny Steps.

FIGURE 6-55: An example of the Hub you see after first entering Creative mode.

To enter any of these areas, simply walk up to one and enter it as your rift destination. For the featured creations, you see the island's description, which includes game type of number of possible players, as in Figure 6-56.

You can also hold down and press the Set Island Code button to enter your own codes. When the Island Codes screen appears, as in Figure 6-57, you enter the numbers in the "0000-0000-0000" field. Chapter 11 has a listing of some great Fortnite island codes to enter and check out.

Of course, you can also customize this Hub screen to a degree, for instance, pressing and holding the Set Rift Destination command when in front of your blank island to change the rift destination. An example of the choices presented when selecting this option is shown in Figure 6-58.

FIGURE 6-56: An example of two featured creations and their descriptions, "The Toilet Paper of Doom Competition" and "Rolling to the Core!"

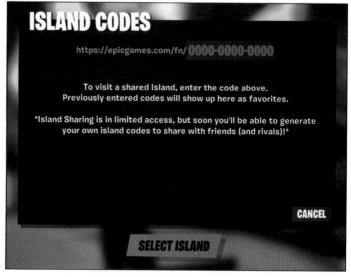

FIGURE 6-57: The Island Codes screen.

FIGURE 6-58: The Island Select screen.

When you land on your island in Creative, you're given essentially a blank slate, as in Figure 6-59. You have unlimited raw materials, unlimited inventory, and an ability to fly. You also have a smartphone in your first inventory slot, which allows you to copy, cut, and delete structures and objects. You can build as much as you want and whatever you'd like on the island as long as there's free memory in the Memory Used display at the bottom-center of the screen.

FIGURE 6-59: The closest thing to a blank canvas with nearly limitless resources in Creative mode.

Settings work more or less the same as in Battle Royale, just with some additional options. Of particular note is My Island, shown in Figure 6-60, which lets you manipulate various Creative mode game and island settings, including your island's name and description.

FIGURE 6-60: My Island options under Settings.

If you ever mess up your island or would simply like to reset your island back to its original state, choose Reset under the Island Tools tab, as shown in Figure 6-61.

FIGURE 6-61: The Island Tools tab.

Your inventory, shown in Figure 6-62, is pre-loaded with some amazing items. Let's take a look at each of the inventory tabs:

>> **Prefabs:** A selection of complex, pre-fabricated buildings. Equipping one of these prefabs adds the building to your inventory as a grenade for placement wherever you throw it. An example is shown in Figure 6-63.

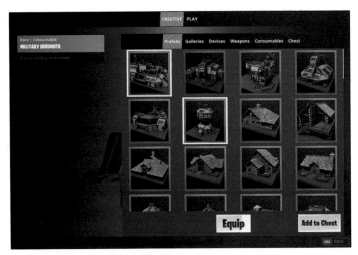

FIGURE 6-62: Creative mode's inventory tabs.

FIGURE 6-63: A prefab Military Behemoth fortress, which can also be edited.

>> **Galleries:** A selection of various pieces, shown in Figure 6-64, that you can build with, including office equipment, letters, numbers, colored shapes, trees, and countless other objects. When you equip one of the galleries, it goes into your inventory as a grenade.

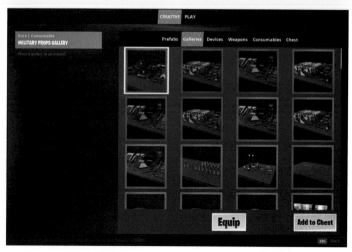

FIGURE 6-64: The Galleries tab.

>> **Devices:** A selection of traps, vehicles, and shooting galleries, as shown in Figure 6-65.

TIP

Adding a vehicle to mess around with from this tab is a great way to practice driving or flying. Of course, you can create your own race tracks or obstacle courses for even more fun as you improve your vehicle skills!

FIGURE 6-65: The Devices tab.

>> **Weapons:** A selection of weapons, grouped by rarity, as shown in Figure 6-66. This is great way to check out weapons that are hard to find in-game or have been otherwise vaulted.

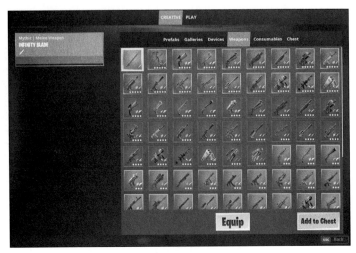

FIGURE 6-66: The Weapons tab.

>> **Consumables:** A selection of various consumables like ammunition, health items, and explosives, as shown in Figure 6-67.

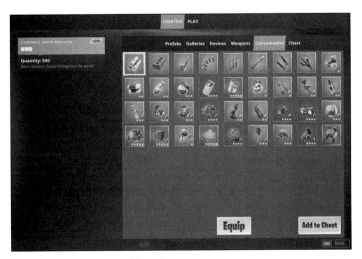

FIGURE 6-67: The Consumables tab.

>> **Chest:** Add items to this tab, shown in Figure 6-68, from any other tab, using the Add to Chest option. After you add items, you can create your own chests or loot llamas for your custom games here.

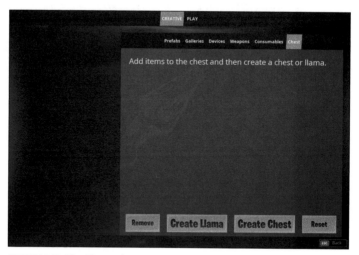

FIGURE 6-68: The Chest tab.

Of course, all of the above is just scratching the surface. Creative mode truly is your own playground with few limits, so get in there and experiment. There's never a wrong way to do anything in Creative mode, so make sure you really explore all the options and have some carefree fun!

Chapter **7**

Getting to Know Battle Pass

The Battle Pass Battle Royale progression system was introduced at the start of Season 2 in December 2017. It rewards players with various cosmetic items that are only available to acquire in that specific Season, but you're then allowed to keep for future Seasons. Although there is a free version of the Battle Pass known as the Free Pass, most of the best items are only available through the premium, paid version. In this chapter, you take a look at the Battle Pass in more detail, including level progression and challenges.

Placing Value on the Battle Pass

A Battle Pass can be purchased at any point during a Season, as shown in Figure 7-1. As of this writing, a Battle Pass costs 950 V-Bucks per Season, which works out to $9.50. If you're in a hurry to progress, you can also purchase a Battle Bundle, which is a Battle Pass plus an automatic 25 tiers of progression, for 4,700 V-Bucks, or $47.00. Of course, as mentioned in Chapter 1, you'll need to purchase a bundle of V-Bucks first and then the Battle Pass, so you're likely to have some V-Bucks left over. You can use the extra V-Bucks to purchase cosmetics, which I cover in the next chapter.

BATTLE PASS OFFERS

SEASON 8 ENDS: 24 Days

40% OFF

OR

BATTLE PASS
Season 8

Ⓥ 950

BATTLE BUNDLE
Battle Pass + 25 tiers!

Ⓥ 2,800 ~~4,700~~

Note: Battle Pass rewards grant no competitive advantage.

FIGURE 7-1: Battle Pass offers from Season 8. Keep an eye out for sales on bundles, like the one shown here for the Battle Bundle.

Epic Games has introduced a way to win a free Battle Pass. Through completion of a specified number of overtime challenges towards the end of a Season, they give away several prizes, including XP, battle stars, wraps, and loading screens. Starting with Season 7, if you completed 13 overtime challenges, the big prize was a free Battle Pass for the next Season, 8. Keep an eye out for similar offers in future Seasons!

The Battle Pass provides a range of cosmetic items that are available to acquire only for that Season, as well as a percentage multiplier to help you quickly get to the next in-game level. Through regular play and completing weekly challenges, you can earn additional cosmetic items in the Battle Pass that have no effect on your in-game level. Instead, you earn Battle Stars to progress through the level tiers in the Battle Pass.

REMEMBER

There is no pay to win in Fortnite. All Battle Rewards are strictly cosmetic and do not affect gameplay.

You start at tier 1 and can go all the way up to tier 100. For every 10 Battle Stars you earn, you go up one level. As with the purchase of the Battle Bundle and its included 25 tiers, you can purchase the next tier should you so choose for 150 V-Bucks, or $1.50.

As you progress through select tiers, you can also earn free V-Bucks, 100 at a time. Although you'll likely want to use your V-Bucks for additional cosmetic items, you can also save these V-Bucks to purchase future Seasons.

TIP

Your account information and V-Bucks are the only things shared between the free game and Save the World. Although the Save the World mode presently costs real money, not V-Bucks, if you happen to also purchase that part of the game, you can also earn V-Bucks there. In fact, there's a lot more potential to earn free V-Bucks in Save the World than there is in the Free Pass in Battle Royale.

The key takeaway with the Battle Pass is that the more you play, the more you'll earn and unlock. Unlockables include outfits, gliders, harvesting tools, pets, backpacks, emotes, sprays, toys, wraps, contrails, music, loading screens, and more. The value of all of the individual cosmetic items you receive far exceeds the cost of the Battle Pass itself.

TIP

Each Battle Pass expires at the end of the Season it was acquired. After a Season is over, you keep all in-game cosmetic rewards earned, but XP boosts end, and you will no longer be able to earn more rewards or complete weekly challenges from that Season.

If you don't have a lot of time to put into the game during a particular Season, then you can enjoy the game just fine without investing in anything more than the Free Pass. If you're able to play on a semi-regular basis, however, and can afford the price, then the Battle Pass is a great way to enhance your experience with some fun items that will never be available again, as well as unique goals to reach for.

Understanding the Progression System

Player progression is measured by two different values: Season level, which is raised through acquiring Season XP, and Battle Pass tier, which increases by accumulating Battle Stars. Season level represents your time playing during the current Season and has the following properties:

>> **Season XP:** Affects Season level. Gained by quality play, including survival time, enemies eliminated, and match placement. Can be awarded directly by completing Battle

Pass challenges and by acquiring Battle Pass tiers. Season XP can be boosted by Battle Pass reward personal XP boosts.

>> **Friend XP:** Boosts the accumulation of Season XP for those you play with, and vice-versa. Only one can be active at a time.

>> **Combo XP:** Boosts both personal XP and friend XP.

>> **Boosts:** All boosts are cumulative.

TIP

To collect enough Battle Stars to earn all Battle Pass rewards without buying tiers, you need to level up and complete daily and weekly challenges. As such, if you want to earn all Battle Pass rewards, you'll want to buy as early in the Season as possible to give yourself enough time.

A Battle Pass tier has the following properties:

>> **Tiers:** Increased through acquisition of Battle Stars. Earning 10 Battle Stars increases the Battle Pass tier by 1, to a maximum level of 100. Tiers can be purchased for 150 V-Bucks each, up to the maximum level of 100.

>> **Battle Stars:** Awarded for completing specific challenges.

>> **Challenges:** Completing daily challenges award five Battle Stars. Completing weekly Battle Pass challenges award five Battle Stars. Completing hard weekly Battle Pass challenges award ten Battle Stars. Some challenges feature multiple stages that award 1–4 Battle Stars per stage.

>> **Leveling Up:** Leveling up a Season level, such as going to level 3, awards two Battle Stars. Leveling up a Season level every multiple of five, such as going to level 25 awards five Battle Stars. Leveling up a Season level every multiple of ten, such as going to level 40, awards ten Battle Stars.

TIP

Purchasing the Battle Pass after unlocking higher tiers will grant all earned Battle Pass rewards.

You can see your Season progress by selecting the Battle Pass tab from the lobby, as shown in Figure 7-2. Let's take a look at the Battle Pass tab:

>> **Tier:** Indicates your current tier, from 1 to 100. The corresponding column shows what you've unlocked. The example

in Figure 7-2 shows that Tier 1 has no unlockable in the Free Pass and four unlockables in the Battle Pass. However, because the Battle Pass was not purchased in the example, those remain unavailable.

>> **Battle Stars:** The first number shows how many Battle Stars have been earned towards the second number goal. It takes ten stars to make it to the next tier of unlockables.

>> **Free Pass:** This row of unlockables is available to every player, even if they did not purchase a Battle Pass. Because this is free, there are far fewer unlockables than with the paid Battle Pass. Unlockables include cosmetic items and free V-Bucks.

>> **Battle Pass:** This row of unlockables is only available to Battle Pass purchasers. Each of the 100 tiers features at least one item to unlock. Unlockables include cosmetic items, free V-Bucks, XP to put towards future Seasons, and more.

>> **Unlockable Description:** By selecting an unlockable's icon in either the Free Pass or Battle Pass row, this area shows a larger image and relevant description so you know exactly what you earned or hope to earn.

>> **Purchase:** If you want to try for the best unlockables, this is how you purchase a Battle Pass. If you don't have enough V-Bucks to complete your order, you'll be taken to V-Bucks purchase options.

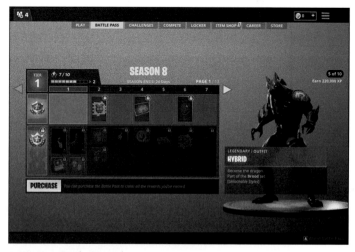

FIGURE 7-2: Battle Pass tab.

As you reach new tiers, you'll be notified and can unlock the item or items for those tiers. Figure 7-3 shows an example of purchasing a Battle Bundle to go straight to tier 26 in Season 8.

FIGURE 7-3: Reaching a new tier notification.

When notified, you can view each of the items and their description, or simply click Collect All and Close to acquire everything available without first reviewing it. Figure 7-4 shows a Battle Pass tab with progress up to tier 26, unlocking everything up to that point in both the Free Pass and Battle Pass rows.

FIGURE 7-4: Battle Pass tab with everything unlocked up to tier 26 in Season 8.

Understanding Daily, Weekly, and Special Challenges

There are four main challenge types: daily, weekly, event, and style. Each challenge type works the same, but features different properties. You can see the current line-up of challenges by selecting the Challenges tab, shown in Figure 7-5.

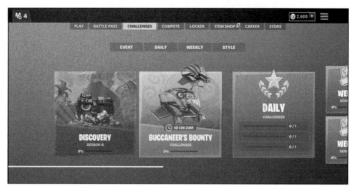

FIGURE 7-5: The Challenges tab.

Clicking on any of the challenge boxes shows what actions are required for completion, as in Figure 7-6.

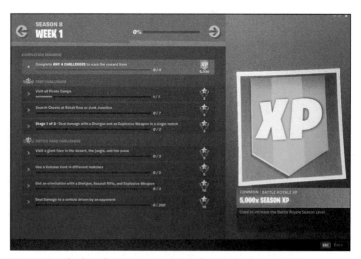

FIGURE 7-6: The list of actions to complete for Week 1 in Season 8.

Daily challenges, shown in Figure 7-7, assign a new series of challenges each day. Completing the daily challenge rewards you with XP and Battle Stars. You can have up to three daily challenges active at one time. To get new daily challenges, you need to first complete your active challenges.

FIGURE 7-7: The daily challenges box.

Weekly challenges are sets of unique challenges that unlock ten weeks during a Season. (See Figure 7-8.) Completing these challenges rewards you with large amounts of Battle Stars that are designed to help you unlock higher tiers. Anyone can complete some of the challenges in each week's set, but you need to own the Battle Pass to complete all of the challenges.

FIGURE 7-8: The weekly challenge boxes.

Event challenges are special challenges that grant loading screen rewards, emotes, or other items, for completing special weekly challenges. (See Figure 7-9.) For each set of event challenges completed, you receive a new loading screen or other reward.

FIGURE 7-9: Event challenge boxes.

Style challenges are special cumulative challenges that grant different outfits or styles for your characters. (See Figure 7-10.) For each set of style challenges completed, you receive a new outfit or style for the character specified.

FIGURE 7-10: Style challenge boxes.

Using Party Assist

Within the Challenges tab, you can turn on Party Assist for a single daily challenge or weekly challenge that may be too hard to pull off by yourself. During a match, when Party Assist is active, your party members can help you complete that challenge.

To use Party Assist, you need to be a member of a party before joining a match. That means you need to team up with from one to three of your friends or family rather than just using the Fill option.

When you're a member of a party, you can then go into the daily or weekly challenge you want help on and select the Party Assist button, as in Figure 7-11.

FIGURE 7-11: Because I'm part of a party, the Party Assist button is active on a Week 1 Season 8 challenge that earns three Battle Stars.

Party Assist can only be used on one daily or weekly challenge at a time and only before the match starts. If the challenge is met by you or one of the other party members, then everyone in the party will receive credit. Encouraging positive teamwork like this is yet another example of Fortnite being a game that's more than just straight up conflict.

Chapter **8**

Enhancing Fortnite Through Premium Cosmetic Items

As you've been reading, Fortnite is a game with many options and a whole heck of a lot of variety. These options and variety extend to how you can personalize the game through cosmetic items like skins, pickaxes, back bling, gliders, umbrellas, contrails, emotes, music, sprays, wraps, emoticons, loading screens, pets, toys, and banners. Although these items have no effect on gameplay, the endless combinations, which you can cycle through and update on a regular basis, let you personalize your character and your character's actions in a way that's uniquely yours. In this chapter, you take a look at filling your locker with this ever-growing list of cosmetic items.

Acquiring Cosmetic Items

As described in Chapter 7, you can unlock unique cosmetic items to add to your locker through regular play in either the Free Pass or Battle Pass. If you don't get XP or V-Bucks each time you move up one of the 100 tiers, you'll get one or more cosmetic items. You can see which items unlock in a particular Free Pass or Battle Pass tier by selecting the Battle Pass tab from the lobby, and then selecting the item from the respective tab to view its description.

In Figure 8-1, I selected the item in the Free Pass row for tier 30, which is an uncommon glider called Cinder. If I reached tier 30 and just had the Free Pass, this is the item I would unlock and have added to my Locker. If I also had the Battle Pass, I would also unlock the uncommon loading screen called The Ice Queen.

FIGURE 8-1: Tier 30 unlocks the uncommon glider called Cinder on the Free Pass row.

There are also other ways to earn free cosmetic items from retailer promotions, special events, or for being an owner of a specific platform. For instance, if you play Fortnite on a PlayStation 4 and have a PlayStation Plus membership, you sometimes get exclusive items, like the Fortnite–PlayStation Plus Carbon Pack in Figure 8-2, which includes a Carbon Commando outfit and Carbon back bling.

These exclusive items show up in your locker and can then be equipped. Figure 8-3 shows the rare outfit called Carbon Commando.

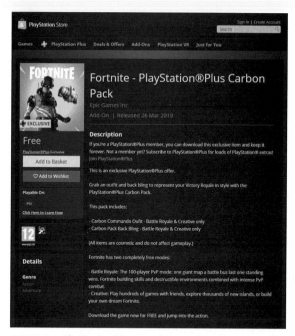

FIGURE 8-2: PlayStation Plus members on the PlayStation 4 sometimes get exclusive items, like the Fortnite–PlayStation Plus Carbon Pack.

FIGURE 8-3: The Carbon Commando outfit.

Figure 8-4 shows the Carbon back bling, a rare glider known as Blue Streak.

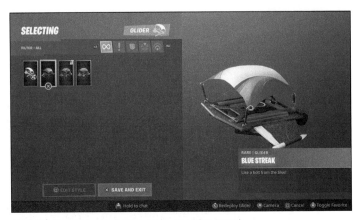

FIGURE 8-4: Carbon back bling known as Blue Streak.

Of course, exclusive skins are not limited to the PlayStation 4. Xbox One and Nintendo Switch owners can also get in on some exclusives, as can users of the Twitch.tv live streaming video platform who upgrade to a Twitch Prime membership, which is great for watching competitive Fortnite matches ad-free.

TIP

Having a Twitch Prime membership, found at `http://twitchprime.com/`, gets you bonus PC games, exclusive in-game content, a channel subscription every month at no additional cost to be used on any partner or affiliate channels, exclusive emotes, a chat badge, and more. Although it normally costs $12.99 per month, or $119 for an annual plan, if you're an Amazon Prime member you can get a Twitch Prime account for free. If you're an Amazon Prime member, visit `https://amzn.to/2DgWQm7` to connect your account.

The last way to acquire cosmetic items is the easiest, and that's by purchasing them in the Item Shop. Let's take a look at the Item Shop in the next section.

Getting to Know the Item Shop

You can purchase cosmetics directly in the Item Shop. You access the Item Shop by selecting the Item Shop tab from the lobby, like shown in Figure 8-5.

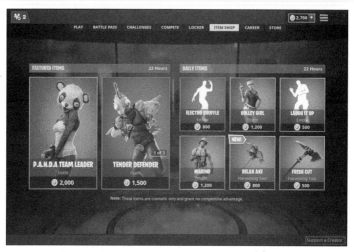

FIGURE 8-5: The Item Shop.

Cosmetics in the Item Shop are purchased with V-Bucks and are broken into two main categories: featured items and daily items. They represent a mix of options, like skins and emotes, but they don't include every type of cosmetic at one time.

Featured items, like the example shown in Figure 8-6, are rotated weekly. The amount of time left to purchase this group of featured items is shown to the right of the Featured Items header.

FIGURE 8-6: The featured items for April 16, 2019.

Daily items, like the example shown in Figure 8-7, are rotated daily. Like with featured items, the amount of time left for daily items is shown to the right of the Daily Items header.

FIGURE 8-7: The daily items for April 16, 2019.

When you select an item to purchase, you're taken to its options and can view it in more detail. Figure 8-8 shows one example for the epic outfit, Tender Defender, which includes the epic back bling, Hatchback, for 1,500 V-Bucks.

To purchase, select Purchase or Purchase Items. If you have enough V-Bucks, they'll be automatically subtracted from your total, like in Figure 8-9. If you don't have enough, you'll be prompted to purchase more V-Bucks.

TIP

Select Purchase Items carefully. If you have enough V-Bucks, the purchase will go through immediately, with no confirmation step. If you accidentally make a purchase, you can go to the Account tab under Settings to request a refund. However, you only get 3 lifetime refund requests per account, so this option should be used only when absolutely necessary.

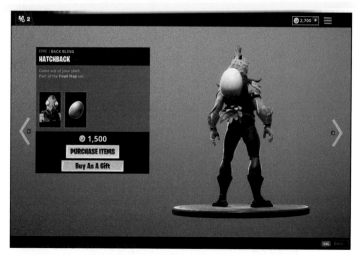

FIGURE 8-8: The combination of the epic outfit Tender Defender and the epic back bling Hatchback costs 1,500 V-Bucks.

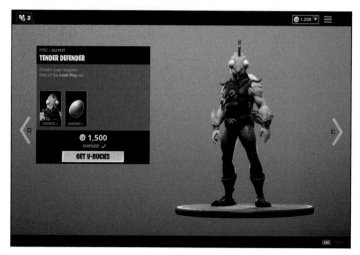

FIGURE 8-9: Purchasing Tender Defender and Hatchback subtracts 1,500 V-Bucks from the previous total of 2,700, leaving 1,200.

If you wish to gift an item to a friend, click the Buy as a Gift button instead of Purchase or Purchase Items. Items you purchase for yourself will show up in your locker, which I discuss in the next section.

Filling Your Locker

After you've received or purchased a new item, you'll be notified one of two ways. If you've received a new item from the Free Pass or Battle Pass, or from some type of redemption offer, you'll be shown the item and prompted to look at and collect it upon entering the lobby, as shown in Figure 8-10.

FIGURE 8-10: Prompt to review and collect the Back Bling Carbon Pack, which was received via a redemption code.

If you purchased an item from the Item Shop, the Locker tab in the lobby is flagged with a yellow exclamation point to indicate the addition of the new item or items, as shown in Figure 8-11.

After selecting the Locker tab, you can see that the new items are flagged in a similar manner, with numbers indicating the amount of new items in a particular category against a yellow background, as shown in Figure 8-12.

Selecting any of these new items in a locker space takes you to the Selecting screen, where you can select the new item or any other item in your locker in that category. Figure 8-13 shows the Outfit options screen.

Before we take a look at the options screen, let's review the elements of the Locker screen, shown in Figure 8-14:

>> **Gear:** The locker spaces from left to right, are: Outfit, Back Bling, Harvesting Tool, Glider, and Contrail.

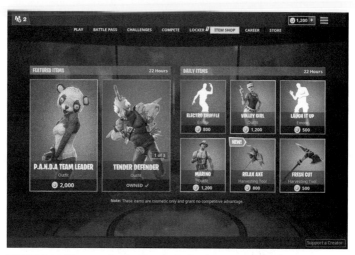

FIGURE 8-11: After purchasing Tender Defender (now marked as owned) and Hatchback, the Locker tab is flagged with a yellow exclamation point.

FIGURE 8-12: There are three new Locker items under Gear, an outfit, back bling, and a glider.

>> **Emote:** The locker spaces from left to right, are Emotes 1 through 6.

>> **Wraps:** The locker spaces from left to right, are: Vehicle Wrap, Assault Rifle Wrap, Shotgun Wrap, SMG Wrap, Sniper Wrap, Pistol Wrap, and Misc Wrap.

>> **Account:** The locker spaces from left to right are: Banner, Music, and Loading Screen.

FIGURE 8-13: The Outfit options screen.

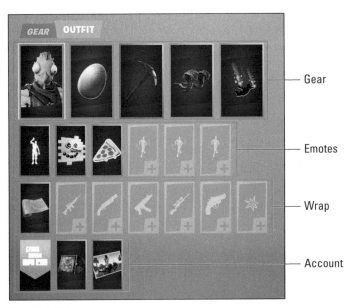

FIGURE 8-14: The Locker screen.

After selecting one of these locker spaces, you are presented with the Selecting screen. Let's review the elements of this screen, shown in Figure 8-15:

>> **Filter:** Choose how to display the list of items, from left to right: All, New, Favorite, Styles, and Reactive.

>> **List of Items:** Displays the items you own by how they're filtered. The first option chooses randomly between favorite items or all owned items if nothing is marked as a favorite.

>> **Edit Style:** Includes only items that have additional options; for instance, additional outfit choices for a particular character will have this option available. Typically, these additional choices open up after achieving a certain XP threshold.

>> **Save and Exit:** Select this option to confirm your selection.

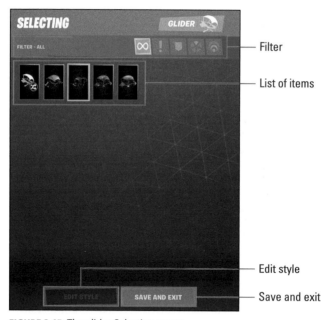

FIGURE 8-15: The glider Selecting screen.

After you have selected your new options from the locker, you're ready to use them in-game. Figure 8-16 shows how distinctive your character can look with just a handful of gear changes.

FIGURE 8-16: Heading towards a landing with the Hybrid outfit, Woodsy Pet back bling, and Sky Serpents glider equipped.

Customizing Character Skins

Character skins, which are stored in the Gear locker under the Outfit options, are the most prominent customization in Fortnite. There are male and female skins, as well as exotic costumes, which make your character stand out like nothing else in the game. This is the easiest way to tell foe from friend, but can also confer other advantages. For instance, some skins make your character thinner, making it easier to hide behind certain objects. Other skins make your character blend in in certain environments. Other skins, like the ones that feature bright colors, make you more prominent, creating a greater challenge.

TIP

Whether labeled as an *outfit*, like in the locker, or referred to as a *skin* or *costume*, it's all just a different way to note your character's appearance and the clothes that your character is wearing.

Some skins can even indicate player skill. For instance, The Reaper skin from Season 3, shown in Figure 8-17, was only available to players who progressed through all 100 tiers.

FIGURE 8-17: The legendary outfit called The Reaper. The resemblance to Keanu Reeves from the 2014 film *John Wick* is purely intentional.

Customizing Pickaxes, Back Bling, and Pets

Pickaxes are stored in the Gear locker under Harvesting Tool, to the right of Back Bling, which includes pets. The standard pickaxe is pretty boring, so this is another favorite to customize. It can take a bit of work to get a pickaxe outside of an outright purchase, but it's well worth it for the new look. Figure 8-18, a rare harvesting tool, Relax Axe, shows how different the pickaxe can be from the standard model.

Because you'll be staring at the back of your character quite a bit, this is a fun area to customize. Besides various backpacks and containers, *back bling* includes pets, like in Figure 8-19. Just like a real pet, these animated figures add a lot of personality to the game.

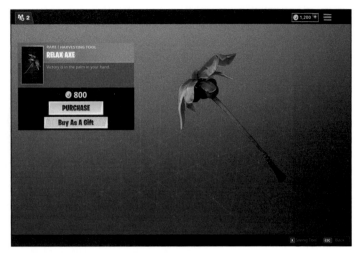

FIGURE 8-18: The rare harvesting tool Relax Axe.

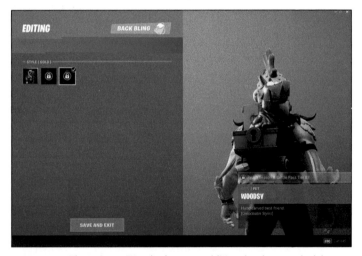

FIGURE 8-19: The epic pet Woodsy has two additional styles to unlock by reaching higher Battle Pass tiers.

Customizing Gliders and Contrails

Gliders are stored in the Gear locker under Glider, to the left of Contrail, where the contrails are stored. Gliders include everything from traditional gliders to umbrellas and paper dragons. Even some fantastic creatures, like the Lavawing, shown in Figure 8-20, make for amazing gliders.

FIGURE 8-20: The legendary glider Lavawing makes for an awesome sight. Warning, you will be noticed!

Contrails, sometimes referred to as *skydiving trails*, are another way to look cool after leaving the Battle Bus. Figure 8-21 shows an example of one of the stranger contrails, the rare Clovers. As with some of the more elaborate gliders, contrails will definitely make you more noticeable on the way down.

FIGURE 8-21: The rare contrail Clovers.

Getting Funky with Emotes, Emoticons, Toys, and Music

Emotes, which have their own category row in the locker, are one of the features that put Fortnite on the map. All the famous Fortnite dance moves are emotes, although emotes can also be any animated action, like vigorous waving, shown in Figure 8-22. These animations are great ways to taunt an opponent or celebrate a victory, and you can have up to six ready to go.

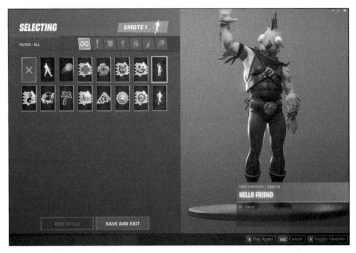

FIGURE 8-22: The uncommon emote Hello Friend features vigorous waving instead of cool dance moves.

TECHNICAL
STUFF

Fortnite's characters are so well animated that they can easily recreate famous dance moves, which has gotten Epic Games into some legal trouble. Dances that mimicked "The Carlton," the "Floss," the "Milly Rock," and others have resulted in legal action.

TIP

Like most in-game actions, emotes make noise, and a lot of it. Save the dancing for when you're clear of danger.

Emoticons and toys, which are also found in the Emotes category row in the Locker, let you show emotion in a different way. Emoticons like Sunshine, shown in Figure 8-23, express a feeling in an emoji-like form.

FIGURE 8-23: The uncommon emoticon Sunshine.

Toys like the rare toy Bouncy Ball, shown in Figure 8-24, let you express a feeling through play. Although toys are useless in battle, using a toy like a basketball usually work a lot like their real-life counterparts and can be a fun way to pass the time between key match events.

Music, which is found under Account in the Music locker, is another celebration feature. It will play after getting a Victory Royale! Although you can't hear it, you can at least see the rare music Ahoy! in Figure 8-25.

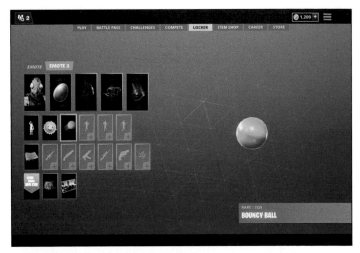

FIGURE 8-24: The rare toy Bouncy Ball.

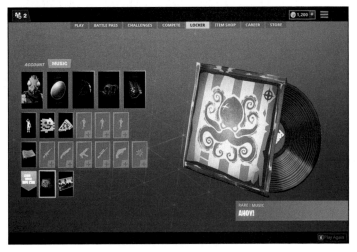

FIGURE 8-25: The image for the rare music Ahoy!.

Applying Sprays, Wraps, Banners, and Loading Screens

Sprays, found in the Emote locker, wraps, found in the Wraps locker, and banners and loading screens, found in the Account locker, are all ways to change the look of existing items.

Sprays like GG Snakes, shown in Figure 8-26, let you *tag*, or spray paint, its image onto walls. It's one of the more interesting and potentially subtle ways to announce your presence to your enemies.

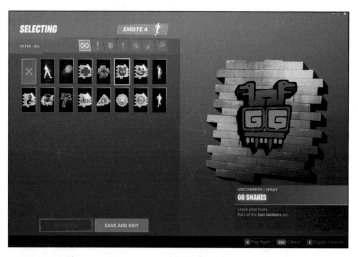

FIGURE 8-26: The uncommon spray GG Snakes.

Wraps let you put a new skin on vehicles, weapons, and other items. Figure 8-27 shows the rare wrap Tropical Camo.

FIGURE 8-27: The rare wrap Tropical Camo.

Selecting Banner brings you to the Edit Banner screen, shown in Figure 8-28. It's at this screen that you change your personal banner's icon and background color. You can select between standard and Battle Royale icon sets. Banners are displayed in matchmaking lobbies, the Party menu, and during some challenges.

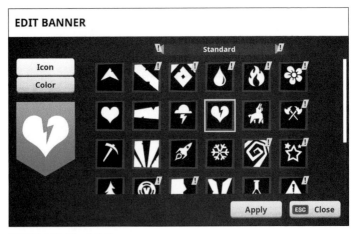

FIGURE 8-28: The Edit Banner screen.

Loading screens change how the loading screens look. Figure 8-29 shows the uncommon loading screen Sgt. Green Clover in action.

FIGURE 8-29: The uncommon loading screen Sgt. Green Clover.

Chapter **9**

Ten Strategies for a Victory Royale

To claim a Victory Royale in Fortnite's Battle Royale, you need to be the last player or team standing. More often than not, reaching these lofty heights is as much about survival as it is about planning or skillful play. Of course, those who win the most know the best ways to survive, but they also have solid plans and engage in skillful play thanks to lots of practice. In this chapter, you look at ten strategies to achieve your own Victory Royale.

Pick Your Battles

The quickest way to lose is to engage any and every enemy you come upon without considering whether or not you're actually ready to survive the fight. Even though it may seem counterintuitive in a fighting game, it's OK to choose not to fight and even to run away. The words *survive* and *survival* have been used many times throughout this book for a reason.

When you spot two players battling it out, hold your fire and stay hidden. When one player eliminates the other, start your attack. It's likely the other player not only will be unable to get their bearings for a few seconds but also will have taken some damage and be weakened from the first fight.

Learn to Aim

Although it's great for gameplay variety, the sheer number of weapons available within Battle Royale means you have to learn different aiming strategies. Generally speaking, the better the weapon, the better its aim. For example, an epic infantry rifle will be a bit easier to aim than a rare infantry rifle.

REMEMBER

Assault rifles and SMGs suffer from bloom, so their bullets don't always hit where you'd expect. This is particularly the case with common versions of these weapons.

The easiest way to practice your aim is to go into Creative mode and fire at a wall, like in Figure 9-1. Observe accuracy at different ranges and how much bloom there is both when aiming and without aiming.

FIGURE 9-1: Aiming and firing a common SMG against a wall to gauge accuracy and bloom.

As a bonus tip, besides knowing how to aim, you'll also want to focus on having a balanced inventory. A popular mix is having an assault rifle in slot 1, a shotgun in slot 2, a sniper rifle in slot 3, explosives in slot 4, and health or shield items in slot 5.

Bandages and med kits improve your HP. Shield potions increase your SP. Slurp juice and chug jugs work on both.

Build Ramps

Battles almost always come down to who can gain the height advantage over the other player. If you can't get higher using existing structures, like in Figure 9-2, quickly build a ramp. Getting to the top of an existing structure is a great way to survey the landscape and spot enemies, but you'll often have to build your own ramps to gain a height advantage or reach otherwise inaccessible places.

FIGURE 9-2: You often have to build your own ramps to gain a height advantage or reach otherwise inaccessible places.

When you attack from a higher elevation, the player you're attacking usually sees less of you, so they have a smaller target. You, on the other hand, can see all of the other player.

TIP

Although building double ramps for safety, as suggested in Chapter 6, is generally faster, putting a wall in front of your ramp also makes it harder for another player to take it out.

Focus on Structural Weak Spots

From simple structures to large forts, anything that gets built has a weakness. If you take out the foundation or base of a structure, the whole structure collapses along with anything, or anyone, on it. A pickaxe is often all you need, but for real speed and maximum efficiency in a battle zone, go for a rocket, as shown in Figure 9-3, grenade, or remote explosive.

FIGURE 9-3: Use explosive weapons to take out structural foundations. They're easy targets and can cause the whole structure to collapse.

Manage Supply Drops

As a match progresses, there will be more supply drops, like the one shown in Figure 9-4. These drops contain powerful legendary weapons, and other supplies that can give you a big advantage. Unfortunately, these supply drops are quite noticeable, so other players are also easily alerted to their presence. Besides falling from the sky as blue crates attached to a balloon and making a beeping sound and other noises, a blue flare indicates where the drop lands.

FIGURE 9-4: A supply drop is a valuable loot crate, but you'll rarely be the only player to notice it.

To more safely explore the contents of a supply drop, first build a small fort around yourself. That then buys you the time needed to sort through the items and update your inventory.

Have Building Materials

Building can provide cover, a place to lay traps, and a way to reach new areas. You can also quickly build structures like a 1x1 fort to hide inside to buy you time to use shield or healing items.

You'll quickly learn that the best players are constantly throwing up everything from walls to complex structures for both protection and to gain the high ground. Especially for the end game, you'll want to have at least 1,500 units of each raw material for maximum versatility.

Know the Map

Learn the map and keep on top of the map changes with each new update. The best players know the best locations with the best chances at quality loot.

Getting to know the various locations also makes it easier to stay ahead of the storm, like in Figure 9-5. When you engage in the inevitable fire fight, a good sense of place and direction helps you both to use the environment to your advantage and to keep away from the storm.

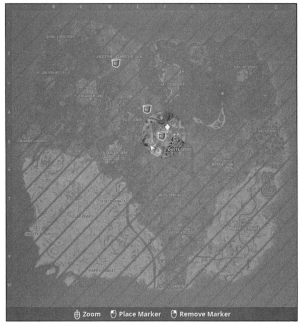

FIGURE 9-5: Knowing the lay of the land allows you to more easily move around the edge of the storm circle.

Let Time Dictate Strategy

You can't use one strategy for the whole game. At the start of a match, you want to land in a sparsely populated area. This can give you a chance to loot, build your inventory, and start to head towards the center of the map, as in Figure 9-6.

FIGURE 9-6: Early on in a match, focus on looting and building up your inventory in a sparsely populated area with scattered buildings, like this one.

For the mid-point of a match, start to seek out and engage enemies. Make liberal use of your building materials and loot fallen opponents.

For the end game, stay in the safety zone of the storm and establish a defensive position. Let the fight come to you. As the number of opponents starts to dwindle to just a handful, look for an opening and get to higher ground. Keep the height advantage as you take out the remaining players.

Coordinate with Your Teammates

When teaming up with other players, communication is key. Be honest about your strengths and weaknesses and insist on the same from your teammates. If, for instance, you're good at sniping, but bad at building, let your teammate know. Placing the best person in their best role can make for the strongest team.

You should try to remain in range of your teammates whenever possible, even when splitting your squad to outflank your opponents. You never know when you'll have to provide support. Take any and every opportunity before a match to discuss strategy and tactics, and make sure you stay in touch as the match unfolds.

The ultimate form of coordination is building a fortress towards the endgame. If everyone has a role and pitches in, you can create far more impressive defensive structures than any one person can on their own.

Practice

It can't be said enough, practice makes perfect. Take advantage of Creative mode and try out all of its options. Play one or more matches of various types every day. Each time you go hands-on with the game, you'll gain a little more experience. Use this book as a guide to identify your weak points and make them strengths through repetition.

TIP

Although getting a Victory Royale is satisfying, always remember that Fortnite is just a game. You'll enjoy yourself much more if you prioritize fun over simply focusing on the work needed to achieve victories.

A great way to identify your weaknesses is by making liberal use of the Replays option under the Career tab in the lobby. This feature lets you watch your recent matches, like in Figure 9-7, and evaluate where you might have gone wrong and what to do better next time. You can also watch other players from your match and learn even more.

FIGURE 9-7: Match replays start from the Battle Bus. You have full control over playback and can even watch from the perspective of other players.

Chapter **10**

Ten Keys to Understanding Save the World

At one time, Fortnite was only Save the World, a paid player-versus-environment (PvE) campaign. With the introduction of the free player-versus-player (PvP) Battle Royale mode and its massive success, Save the World took a back seat. That doesn't mean Save the World is a bad game, however. Quite the contrary. Both game modes share many of the same gameplay traits, but Save the World is story-driven and designed around a solo or cooperative play experience. All PvP combat is reserved for the free Battle Royale game. In this chapter you take a closer look at ten keys to understanding Save the World, which is available to PC, Mac, PlayStation 4, and Xbox One owners.

REMEMBER

As of this writing and barring any special offers, the Standard Founder's Pack for Save the World costs $39.99. Although Epic Games has stated that Save the World will become free at some point, they plan to delay availability in that format until they've sufficiently expanded the in-game story.

Mandatory Tutorial

Save the World is set in a near-future Earth where a worldwide storm, shown in Figure 10-1, has caused 98 percent of the world's population to disappear, replaced with *husks*, zombie-like creatures that attack the survivors. You and three other players, either humans or computer-generated teammates, work towards a common goal on various missions.

FIGURE 10-1: The opening cut scene shows the storm that ravaged the Earth.

You need to fight against the storm, rescue survivors, build structures, craft weapons, find loot, and upgrade and expand a shield device to protect your base of operations.

After the opening cut-scenes establish the story and describe the need for a commander, you, you're immediately tasked with taking down an advancing group of husks, as shown in Figure 10-2.

FIGURE 10-2: Showing no mercy, Save the World places you in an immediate firefight with enemy husks.

As in Battle Royale, aim for the heads! If you succeed in taking out all of the husks, your next step will be to find a way out of the caves. Head towards the yellow checkpoint symbol, like shown in Figure 10-3.

FIGURE 10-3: The yellow exclamation point at the center of the screen indicates the next destination.

After you reach the mine cart, as shown in Figure 10-4, destroy it with your pickaxe. Continue following the rest of the tutorial, using the skills you learned from Battle Royale, including building. You'll also learn some new skills, like crafting, where you can harvest materials to build weapons. Good luck!

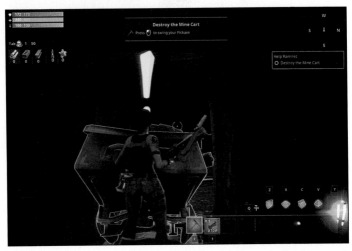

FIGURE 10-4: Destroy the mine cart and continue with the rest of the tutorial.

Mission Structure Based on Objectives and Quests

After you get past its tutorials, Save the World involves mission-based objectives and quests where you defend locations against enemy husks or seek out stranded survivors. For defense missions, you'll be harvesting materials to make needed items and setting up and building fortifications. When you're ready, you'll need to defend your base.

The map, like shown in Figure 10-5, is randomly generated for each mission, save for the map where your home base is located.

You'll return to your storm shield on your home base's map to increase the radius of the shield's influence.

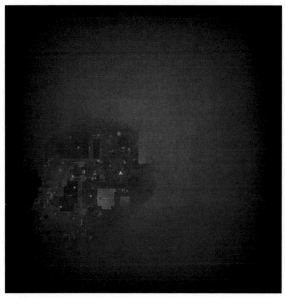

FIGURE 10-5: The Save the World map works on the same grid-based system as in Battle Royale, but it is randomly generated. As you explore, more of the map gets revealed.

V-Bucks and Llamas

Just like in Battle Royale and its related modes, V-Bucks can be spent in Save the World. However, items bought in Save the World do not transfer to Battle Royale and vice-versa.

In Save the World, you can purchase llama pinatas, like shown in Figure 10-6, which contain weapon and trap schematics, XP, new heroes, and more.

FIGURE 10-6: An upgrade llama.

Heroes

There are four main hero classes in Save the World, which are described as follows:

>> **Constructor:** Shown in Figure 10-7, this is the strongest in building, defending structures, and crowd control. This hero class has 18 standard subclasses, each with unique perks and bonuses.

>> **Ninja:** Shown in Figure 10-8, this is the strongest in melee combat and quick movement. This hero class has 19 standard subclasses, each with unique perks and bonuses.

>> **Soldier:** Shown in Figure 10-9, this is the strongest in ranged combat and the use of guns and grenades. This hero class has 19 standard subclasses, each with unique perks and bonuses.

>> **Outlander:** Shown in Figure 10-10, this is the strongest in resource collection, scouting, and crowd control. This hero class has 19 standard subclasses, each with unique perks and bonuses.

Hero subclasses determine the abilities, hero perks, and squad bonuses received as the character is upgraded and evolved. You can choose hero perks to maximize the effectives of your gameplay style and even stack heroes to increase weapon damage.

FIGURE 10-7: Constructor hero class.

FIGURE 10-8: Ninja hero class.

FIGURE 10-9: Solder hero class.

FIGURE 10-10: Outlander hero class.

Command Center

The Command Center lets you track every aspect of your heroes. Apply XP boosts, check notices and alerts, and review your Power and Account levels through each of your heroes to keep tabs on all of your available options.

Weapons

There are two categories of weapons in Save the World: ranged and melee. Ranged weapons include: assault rifles, explosive weapons, pistols, shotguns, and sniper rifles.

Melee weapons include: axes, clubs, hardware, scythes, spears, and swords.

Like heroes, each weapon has a subclass that determines performance.

Weapon schematics are used to craft a specific weapon. Crafting requires the correct number of materials listed on the schematic, like the example for a common assault rifle shown in Figure 10-11.

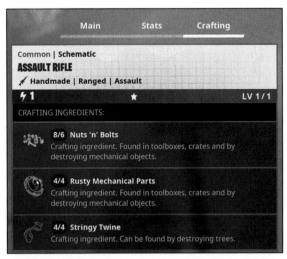

FIGURE 10-11: The schematic for a common assault rifle listing the required crafting ingredients.

Unlike in Battle Royale, weapons wear out and break over time. After it's broken, the weapon can be recycled to reclaim a portion of its original crafting materials.

Traps

There are three categories of traps in Save the World: wall traps, floor traps, and ceiling traps. Traps work the same as in Battle Royale, with defensive traps that damage or disrupt enemies, such as the ceiling Electric Field trap shown in Figure 10-12, and utility traps that perform a function like healing.

FIGURE 10-12: The ceiling Electric Field trap targets enemies in a 3 x 3 tile radius.

Just as with weapons, trap schematics are used to craft a specific trap and traps wear out and break over a set number of triggers.

Player Statistics

The acronym F.O.R.T. represents the four types of player statistics, each of which can be increased by 1 percent per point:

>> **(F)ortitude:** Health and health regeneration.

>> **(O)ffense:** Ranged and melee weapon damage.

>> **(R)esistance:** Shield and shield generation.

>> **(T)ech:** Trap, ability, and gadget damage, as well as healing.

F.O.R.T. statistics total the bonuses awarded by survivor squads and skills, and are found under the Squads tab. There are two types of survivors in Save the World: lead survivors and survivors. Lead survivors, like the doctor female leader shown in Figure 10-13, affect a larger percentage of F.O.R.T. statistics and are slotted into the Leader slot for each squad.

FIGURE 10-13: A doctor female leader gets slotted into the Leader slot for each squad.

Inserting survivors into survivor squads grants F.O.R.T. statistics by squad type:

TIP

To save time or eliminate the task from your to do list, use the Autofill Survivors option to automatically manage your survivors and squads.

>> **(F)ortitude:** EMT Squad and Training Team.

>> **(O)ffense:** Fire Team Alpha and Close Assault Squad.

>> **(R)esistance:** Scouting Party and Gadgeteers.

>> **(T)ech:** Corps of Engineering and The Think Tank.

Your Power, which is the number in the upper-left corner next to the lightning bolt, as shown in Figure 10-14, is a summary of your F.O.R.T. statistics mixed with the boosts from your survivor squads. The higher the number, the more potent your hero and abilities.

FIGURE 10-14: Your starting Power level.

Unlike your Account level, which only goes up, your Power level can be both boosted or reduced depending upon your actions at any one time, including mission type, party make-up, and active perks.

Upgrade Points

All rewards are associated with your account level. Upgrade points are awarded based on your current account level. These points can be spent to unlock improved pickaxes, building health, gadgets, storage capacity, and other improvements in the Upgrades page.

Monsters

As you progress through Save the World, you'll not only encounter husks, but other monster types. Let's take a look at some of these monsters:

>> **Elemental monsters:** High-level enemies that include the following:

- *Fire monster:* Weak against water weapons and does double damage to wood structures.

- *Nature monster:* Weak against fire weapons and does double damage to metal structures.

- *Water monster:* Weak against nature weapons and does double damage to stone structures.

>> **Husk:** Most common monsters that attack on sight. There are a variety of husk types with different appearances and attacks.

>> **Mimics:** Conceal themselves as treasure chests and do bite damage.

>> **Mist monsters:** The second most-common monster type that attacks on sight. These large monsters create openings for smaller husks to attack. Figure 10-15 shows a flinger mist monster, which throws husks towards your base.

>> **Trolls:** Can pass through walls and steal materials.

FIGURE 10-15: A flinger mist monster.

Chapter **11**

Ten Great Fortnite Creative Codes

Fortnite's Creative mode is the perfect sandbox to flex your creative muscles. It's also a great place to check out what others have come up with. Thanks to Fortnite's incredible popularity, there are tons of great custom creations available to play around with. As mentioned in Chapter 6, simply head to a featured rift, hold down and press the Set Island Code button, and enter the code to start playing. The ten Creative codes featured in this chapter are some of the best custom creations available.

Choice! A Choose Your Own Adventure Map

Code: 5170-0305-7409

Choose Your Own Adventure books have been hugely popular since their introduction in the 1970s. In these books, the reader takes the role of the protagonist and makes decisions that affect the outcome of the story. MIXER-ONSIDEDAFF has taken this concept to Fortnite with Choice! A Choose Your Own Adventure Map. On this island, shown in Figure 11-1, you have to make your way through an epic adventure where every choice you make will impact the type of ending you reach! An interesting narrative and lots of puzzles make for a compelling experience.

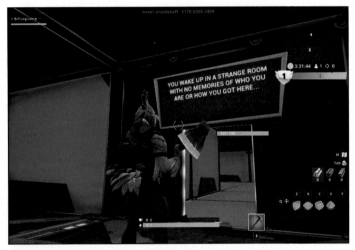

FIGURE 11-1: The opening room of Choice! A Choose Your Own Adventure Map.

Freaky Flights

Code: 1743-0750-4752

Teams of two battle it out with planes, battleships, legendary weapons, and unlimited ammo in SENIX's action-packed creation. A scene from this island is shown in Figure 11-2.

FIGURE 11-2: Aboard a battleship in Freaky Flights.

Hoo Baller Pinball Island

Code: 4573-9507-5308

In Fortnite, a *baller* is a ball-like vehicle. HOOSHEN has taken this basic concept to its logical conclusion, creating a pinball course with a clever scoring system. The opening scene of this island is shown in Figure 11-3.

FIGURE 11-3: Inside a baller in the opening scene of Hoo Baller Pinball Island.

Lundle's Puzzle Escape!

Code: 1039-4421-2809

Escape rooms are popular live action adventure games where a group of players solve a series of puzzles through a combination of strategy and simple trial-and-error. LUNDLEYT has brought this concept to Fortnite, creating five complex multi-step puzzle stages that include all terrain karts, better known as ATKs. The opening scene of this island is shown in Figure 11-4.

FIGURE 11-4: The opening scene of Lundle's Puzzle Escape!.

Raft Wars

Code: 9026-2925-8175

AZALIAK_IPHONE's Raft Wars brings naval warfare to Fortnite. Battle it out on dangerous waters with nine rafts and pirate cannons. The opening scene of this island is shown in Figure 11-5.

FIGURE 11-5: The opening scene of Raft Wars.

Rainbow Road

Code: 2668-3299-2351

The Super Nintendo classic Super Mario Kart came out in 1992, launching a series that's still going strong today and changing the world of video game racing forever. FALCONSTRIKE1998's Rainbow Road is a surprisingly faithful and feature-packed adaptation of one of Super Mario Kart's most iconic courses. The opening scene of this island is shown in Figure 11-6.

FIGURE 11-6: The opening scene of Rainbow Road.

Larger islands, like Rainbow Road, can take extra time to load. Your patience will be rewarded soon enough!

Snipers vs Runners

Code: 7352-4203-8482

Whether you enjoy using sniper weapons, evading sniper fire, or both, there's plenty to love about BLUDRIVE's Snipers vs Runners. Team 1 plays the runners and Team 2 plays the snipers. If the runners make it to the end, they win! A portion of the course is shown in Figure 11-7.

FIGURE 11-7: The runners not only have the snipers to deal with, but also obstacles!

Space Parkour!

Code: 1986-0450-3000

Parkour, where a person tries to get from one point to another in the fastest and most efficient way possible regardless of obstacles, makes for a great video game concept. Fortunately, Fortnite's game engine is well-suited to parkour-style gaming. With floating ice platforms and plenty of coins to collect, HIGH-POXIA has done a great job of bringing the concept to Fortnite with Space Parkour!. The opening scene of this island is shown in Figure 11-8.

FIGURE 11-8: The opening scene of Space Parkour!.

Tony Hawk's Pro Skater's "Warehouse"

Code: 9977-2394-8492

Tony Hawk's Pro Skater set a new standard for skateboarding video games when it was first released for the Sony PlayStation in 1999. The first level of that legendary game took place in a warehouse, which has been recreated for Fortnite by PSYCHECLOPS. In Tony Hawk's Pro Skater's "Warehouse", use a hoverboard-like driftboard to collect coins, puzzle pieces, and toilet paper, as well as just zoom around the course, like in Figure 11-9.

FIGURE 11-9: Shredding it on a driftboard.

Weezer World!

Code: 1349-5880-2084

Although an island themed to American rock band, Weezer, might not sound that exciting to non-fans, CRE8's Weezer World! just might change their mind. It's a theme park with puzzles, collectibles, and different attractions that include driftboarding, a roller-coaster, a shooting gallery, and parkour. And if you're a fan of the band, a neat bonus is that Weezer's music plays in the background! The opening scene of this island is shown in Figure 11-10.

FIGURE 11-10: The opening scene of Weezer World!.

Chapter **12**

Ten Ways to Enjoy Fortnite When Not Playing

ortnite is a genuine cultural phenomenon, so it's no surprise there are tons of other ways to get your Fortnite fix, even when you're not playing the actual game. This chapter covers ten fun ways to enjoy Fortnite, no controller needed!

Action Figures and Playsets

If you'd like to use a bit of imagination to recreate some in-game battles, a fun choice is the line of four-inch action figures from

Jazwares. Each figure is based on a popular outfit and features 19 points of articulation and a pickaxe or weapon. There are also playsets, like the Fortnite Turbo Builder Set shown in Figure 12-1, and Fortnite Loot Chest Collectibles, that feature weapons and other items to further outfit your action figures. And if you're looking for something a bit larger and a bit higher quality, McFarlane Toys has seven-inch action figures.

Source: Amazon.com

FIGURE 12-1: The Jazwares Turbo Builder Set comes with two action figures, Jonesy and Rave, and lets you link together the building materials just about any way you'd like.

Apparel

Whether you wear child or adult sizes, there are all kinds of T-shirts, pajamas, underwear, and other apparel available to show off your love of Fortnite. The Mad Engine Fortnite Dance Dance T-shirt, like the one shown in Figure 12-2, is particularly popular, but there are all kinds of designs and styles to choose from.

FIGURE 12-2: The Mad Engine Fortnite Dance Dance T-shirt.

Board Games

As amazing as Fortnite is, it can seem unapproachable to the uninitiated. One clever way to ease someone into the Fortnite universe is through ubiquitous board game, Monopoly. Hasbro's Monopoly: Fortnite Edition, shown in Figure 12-3, is fun for both fans of Monopoly and fans of Fortnite because it features the venerable board game's ruleset with locations, cards, and tokens themed to the video game.

Calendars, Journals, and Notebooks

Fortnite has an ever-expanding cast of colorful characters and rich environments, which are a perfect decoration for calendars, journals, and notebooks. An example, the Readerlink Fortnite Official Journal, is shown in Figure 12-4.

FIGURE 12-3: Hasbro's Monopoly: Fortnite Edition.

FIGURE 12-4: The Readerlink Fortnite Official Journal.

Collectibles

Sure, there are Fortnite-themed mugs, speakers, and keychains, but you haven't really made it until you've been immortalized as a collectible figurine. Funko makes some of the most widely available of these collectibles as part of their Vynl. and POP! series. A popular example is the Funko POP! Games: Fortnite – Black Knight, shown in Figure 12-5.

Source: Amazon.com

FIGURE 12-5: Funko POP! Games: Fortnite – Black Knight.

Costumes

Looking for something a bit more involved than a T-shirt or pajamas? Why not go full Fortnite and score one of an impressive range of costumes? If that's a bit too much, you can always just get a cool Fortnite mask, like the Spencer Gifts Drift Mask – Fortnite, shown in Figure 12-6.

FIGURE 12-6: Spencer Gifts Drift Mask – Fortnite.

Home Goods

Fortnite-themed merchandise works in every room of the house, including the living room and bedroom. From Fortnite sheet sets to blankets and pillows, including the Target Fortnite Supply Llama Gotta Get the Juice throw pillow shown in Figure 12-7, you can have both style and comfort.

FIGURE 12-7: Target Fortnite Supply Llama Gotta Get the Juice throw pillow.

NERF Blasters and Super Soakers

Since 1992, Hasbro has made a popular line of toy guns known as NERF Blasters, which shoot foam projectiles. Starting in 2002, Hasbro has also produced NERF Super Soakers, a series of powerful waterguns. The inevitable marriage of NERF Blasters and Super Soakers with the Fortnite brand has produced some of the coolest functional toy guns around, including the NERF Fortnite SP-L Elite Dart Blaster, shown in Figure 12-8.

Source: Amazon.com

FIGURE 12-8: NERF Fortnite SP-L Elite Dart Blaster.

Plushies

Fortnite is filled with wacky and cute characters, which are naturals for plush toys. Perhaps no Fortnite character is cuter, though, than the Loot Llama, who is immortalized in the seven-inch Jazwares Fortnite Llama Loot plush, shown in Figure 12-9.

Source: Amazon.com

FIGURE 12-9: Jazwares Fortnite Llama Loot plush.

Spectating

Fortnite is almost as fun to watch as it is to play. Fortunately, there are plenty of ways to watch, including on YouTube and Twitch.tv. Fortnite even has its own dedicated channel on Twitch, which you can find at `https://www.twitch.tv/fortnite`. There you can check out popular clips and channels, as well as any special live events, like the Fortnite World Cup. Across 2019, Epic Games has doled out an amazing $100,000,000 in prize money, so you can bet these live events get competitive! And who knows, if you keep referring to this book and watching how the world's best players compete, some of that prize money may be in your future as well.

Good luck, but above all, keep having fun!

Index

C

projectiles, aiming, 85–90

PSYCHECLOPS, 205–206

pump shotgun, 75, 76

Purchase (Battle Pass tab), 149

purchasing
  accessories, 46–50
  cosmetic items, 160
  gamepads, 48–49
  headsets, 49–50
  keyboards, 48
  mouse, 47
  V-Bucks, 17–18

PvF (player-*versus*-environment) campaign, 14, 185

PvP (player-*versus*-player) Battle Royale mode, 14, 185

pyramids
  about, 107
  editing, 126–129
  HP (hit points) for, 109

Q

Question Mark icon (Settings screen), 26

quests, mission structure based on, 188–189

R

Raft Wars, 202–203

Rainbow Road, 203–204

ramp pyramid, creating, 127–128

ramps
  about, 107
  building, 179–180
  double, 130
  editing, 121–126

HP (hit points) for, 109

panic, 131

scissor, 132

rarity, as weapon characteristic, 74

raw materials
  about, 101–103
  harvesting, 104–107

Razer DeathAdder Elite gaming mouse, 47

Razer Raiju Pro gaming controller, 48

Readerlink Fortnite Official Journal, 211–212

The Reaper skin, 166–167

Reboot Van, 92

refund requests, 160

Region section (Game tab), 29

registering Fortnite accounts, 9–11

Relax Axe, 167

reload time, as weapon characteristic, 75

Remember icon, 3

remote explosives, 89

Replays option, 184

Report Player (Settings screen), 26

Reset Building Choice, 30

Retail Row, 67

revolver, 76

ridge pyramid, creating, 126–127

Rift-to-go, 99

rocket launchers, 79, 85, 180

Rotate, 109

S

safe zone, 57–58

Salty Springs, 69

Save and Exit (Selecting screen), 165

About the Author

Bill Loguidice is a critically acclaimed technology author and journalist, as well as co-founder and managing director for the online publications *Armchair Arcade* and *fullSTEAMahead365*, and co-founder of the creative services firm Armchair Creative Services. He is a noted videogame and computer historian and subject matter expert who has worked on more than a dozen books, including *Motorola Atrix For Dummies* and *Wii Fitness For Dummies*.

Author's Acknowledgments

I'd like to thank the team at Wiley for their support on this project, particularly my direct contacts, Ashley Coffey and Chris Morris. And, as always, thanks to my literary agent, Matt Wagner, for setting it all up.

Dedication

I dedicate this book to my family, but Eva in particular. Here's one for you, Evangeline!

Publisher's Acknowledgments

Acquisitions Editor: Ashley Coffey

Project Editor: Christopher Morris

Copy Editor: Christopher Morris

Technical Editor: Connor Morris

Production Editor:
Mohammed Zafar Ali

Cover Images: © Farknot_Architect/
Getty Images, Screenshot:
Courtesy of Bill Loguidice